Emmanuel Kenners

The Japanese martyrs

A brief sketch of the lives and martyrdom of the Franciscan saints, who were

canonized at St. Peter's, in Rome, by Pope Pius IX., on Whit-Sunday, June 8th, 1862

Emmanuel Kenners

The Japanese martyrs
A brief sketch of the lives and martyrdom of the Franciscan saints, who were canonized at St. Peter's, in Rome, by Pope Pius IX., on Whit-Sunday, June 8th, 1862

ISBN/EAN: 9783741175749

Manufactured in Europe, USA, Canada, Australia, Japa

Cover: Foto ©Andreas Hilbeck / pixelio.de

Manufactured and distributed by brebook publishing software (www.brebook.com)

Emmanuel Kenners

The Japanese martyrs

THE

JAPANESE MARTYRS:

OR,

A BRIEF SKETCH

OF THE

LIVES AND MARTYRDOM

OF THE

FRANCISCAN SAINTS,

WHO WERE

CANONIZED AT ST. PETER'S, IN ROME,

BY

POPE PIUS IX.,

ON WHIT-SUNDAY, JUNE 8TH, 1862.

BY THE

REV. FATHER EMMANUEL KENNERS, O.S.F.

"Moriar amore amoris tui, qui amore amoris mei dignatus es mori."
ST. FRANCIS OF ASSISIUM.

MANCHESTER :
ALEX. IRELAND & CO., PRINTERS, PALL MALL COURT.
1862.

CHAPTER I.

INTRODUCTION.

HUMILITY is the foundation of the Christian life: hence the world and religion have been always antagonistic. Not because religion is opposed to man's happiness, but because the pride of the intellect and the pride of the heart have always risen in rebellion against revealed dogmas and the ethics of the Gospel of Christ. To cure this fatal blindness, the Saviour not only clothed Himself in our flesh, but lovingly assumed the poverty of the most humble of His creatures. For He wished not only to solace the afflicted, but to rectify our notions, by teaching us to believe most firmly that we are only sojourners here, placed on this globe, as in a preparatory school, to be moulded and fitted for an eternal state of existence, where sorrow has no place, and joy no end. His own appearance amongst us was in poverty and humiliation; and the instruments whom he has selected, in every age of the Church's existence, for the accomplishment of His great designs, have invariably been such as to convince men of good-will, that they were His ambassadors, and that the work in which they were engaged was truly His. That man with finite intellect, and that but rarely cultivated, should refuse submission, is a fatal result of primeval transgression.

And yet a little reflection would suffice to rectify our notions, and lead us to submission. For God, in creating us, and placing us on this earth, must have had a set purpose, and He must have left adequate means at our disposal for ascertaining what that purpose was. Hence, two things are placed beyond all controversy: God must have spoken, and He must have communicâted what He spoke, for our rule and guidance. Since He is the Eternal Wisdom, and is all goodness and love, He never would have created us responsible beings without enabling us to learn with facility by what means we might worship Him and obey His law. In every age of the world He has deputed His ministers to remind us of our duties; and by the power of His grace He has from time to time raised up from amongst ourselves, glorious examples for our imitation, to convince us that if of ourselves we can do nothing pleasing in His sight, we can do all things with His divine assistance. As God is one and is immutable, so the religion of God must be always one and immutable. To suppose that there can be more than one true religion, is to suppose, what is both paradoxical and blasphemous, that there can be more than one true God. As the human intellect is capable of gradual developments, so the religion of God has undergone gradual developments. But as man is incapable of organic change, so the religion of God is incapable of organic change. The change in man from infancy to puberty, and from puberty to manhood, does not destroy his identity. And the developments which religion has undergone, under the Patriarchs, under Moses, and under Christ, have not destroyed her identity; but, on the contrary, in the different phases of her being, we behold the wisdom of her Author, and see the foundations of her perpetual indestructibility. The reasoning of the renowned St. Vincent, of Lerins, upon the subject, is both solid and beautiful. In the xxviii. chapter of his " Commonitorium," he says :—" But here, then, perhaps it will be asked, ' *What, must there be no proficiency, no improvement of religion in the Christian Church?'* Yes, without doubt, very great; for, who can be so envious to man, so professed an enemy of God, as to labour against such improvements? But, then, we must be sure not to change Christianity, under the pretence of improving it : for, to improve anything to the utmost, is to enlarge that thing to the just standard and perfection of its own nature. On the other hand, it is not so properly an improvement, as a change, when we mix something heterogeneous, and the thing ceases to be what it was, in its own nature, and becomes of another kind. It is the duty, then, of all in general, and of every individual Christian in particular, in every age of the Church, to increase and grow in understanding, knowledge, and wisdom ; but, then, they must continue Christians still, the growth must be natural, in one and the same kind of faith, in the same meaning, and in the same mind."

" Let this, then, be our rule, let our minds grow in religion, just as our bodies grow in bulk ; for these, though by degrees they unfold and disclose that perfect symmetry of parts, which they had before in little, though they expand and enlarge their size, yet continue to be the very same bodies they always were. There is a great difference, it is true, between the flower of youth and the maturity of age ; yet the man in his youth, and the man in his old age, is the same man still; and though his stature and looks may be altered, yet his nature is the same, and he the very same person he always was. Our members, in our infancy are small, and in our youth large, but for all this, they are the very same members still; for infants have all the component parts of man, and whatever we find produced by the maturity of age, is nothing but an evolution of that which was in the seed; so that there is no new perfection of essence accruing to man, by growing old, he *then* has that only in large, which he had *before* in little."

"Hence, therefore, it is evident, that this only is the just and regular way of increasing the established and beautiful order of growth, when we always retain the same parts and the same figure; and time does nothing else but spin out those principles to their due proportion, which the wisdom of our Creator formed in us from the beginning. *But now, if the human shape should become deformed and at length degenerate into a figure of another kind, or there should be any addition to, or any diminution from, the just number of parts, such a change, I say, must necessarily either ruin the whole body, or make it monstrous, or certainly weaken it in a very great measure.* In the same manner it is that the Christian religion must grow; this is the rule it must follow in its proficiency and improvement: it is to be corroborated by years, it is by degrees to increase to its just breadth and height; but in all this time of growing, it must continue pure and entire, and perfectly the same in, all its several parts and members. But, to speak more plainly, the Christian faith must never admit of any alteration in its essential properties, either by augmentation or diminution, but its definition, or essence, must always continue one and the same." In fact, as the same Holy Father writes in the beginning of the same book, chapter iii., the doctrines of Christ are only such "*as we find to have been believed in all places, at all times, and by all the faithful.*"

The prophet, Daniel, chap. ii., in his interpretation of the mysterious dream of Nebuchodonosor, briefly, but sublimely, gives the glorious history of the chaste Spouse of Christ, His One, Holy, Catholic and Apostolical Church. *She is* the "*little stone cut out of the mountain without hands*," but *she* is to become "*a great mountain, and to fill the whole earth.*" *She is* to rise upon the ruins of the great mighty Roman Empire, which had nearly swallowed up the whole of the three preceding great monarchies; but as she was not of human device, but the work of God, her sway was to extend to the very limits of the earth, and her duration was to be not only commensurate with all time, but to run coeval with the years of eternity. Vain philosophy, human passion, infernal malice, were to wage perpetual war against her; but God's veracity stands pledged for her security, and their discomfiture. And in order to baffle the tortuous windings of sophistry, and to silence the "*non serviam*" of the depraved human heart, he has, in the persons of His Prophets, His Apostles, His Preachers, and His Saints, chosen "*the weak-things of this world to confound the strong, and the foolish things of this world to confound the wise.*"

To enumerate the many heroes whom God has miraculously raised up in the Church, in every age and country, would be an Herculean task, for the history of the world would have to be written; and though the world itself "*could not contain the books that would be written*," yet the task would remain unfinished, since the human memory could not retain the recollection of all the wonders which God has wrought in His Saints, nor the human intellect find adequate language to pourtray the extent of God's loving-kindness to his fallen creatures. . .

Yes, God is truly "*wonderful in his Saints*," for they have conquered kingdoms, subdued the powers of hell, snatched myriads from perdition, and conducted them to paradise. They have humanised savage and barbarous peoples, and have spread amongst them the blessings of evangelical education. They have conducted them within the vestibule of science, and imbued them with a knowledge of that Christian civilisation which is both the child and the hand-maid of Catholicity. On the solemn Feast of Penti-cost, June 8th, in this year of grace 1862, the illustrious supreme Pontiff, Pius IX., surrounded by members of the episcopal body from all parts of the world, and by thousands of the clergy, both secular and regular, and of the people, in that masterpiece of human skill, the magnificent Church of St. Peter, the Apostle, and beneath its lofty and ponderous dome, exercising that amplitude of plenary power which, with the keys, he received, through Peter, from Christ, has solemnly enrolled amongst the Saints twenty-four of those illustrious champions whom, in his might, he has raised up, from time to time, to promote His honour, and to labour for man's salva-tion. · Twenty-three of the number were members of the Seraphical Order of St. Francis, whose lives were formed upon the model of their holy founder, and whose blood, shed in defence of God and His Holy Church, has watered the ungrateful soil of Japan. What a grand spectacle was presented to view on that solemn day, in that sacred temple ! Never was the imposing and mystic rite of Canonisation accompanied with such religious pomp and ceremony. Never did so large an assemblage of Bishops and other digni-taries meet together within the walls of the Holy City. Never was festival surrounded with so bright a halo of glory. Never were more visibly present to men of good-will the interventions of our loving and benefi-cent God than at this ever-memorable time, when, by means of an impious league entered into by men of the Jacobinical and anti-Christian school with the powers of darkness, the flood-gates of impiety and licentiousness have been opened to engulph dynasties and the everlasting Church, in a common ruin.

In the following pages, an interesting account will be given of the holy Martyrs whom the Church has raised upon her altars. A concise but clear description will be given of Japan, its people and its customs. We shall treat of the introduction of Christianity into that remote region—the progress it made—the persecutions it endured—and its final expulsion. And though we have primarily had in view the lives and martyrdom of those glorious heroes, we propose to make our book one of general utility, in which God's ways to man will be triumphantly vindicated, and the authority of His holy Church placed upon an unassailable basis.

CHAPTER II.

A DESCRIPTION OF JAPAN, WITH A CONCISE ACCOUNT OF
THE MISSIONARY LABOURS OF ST. FRANCIS XAVIER, THE
APOSTLE OF THE EAST INDIES.

THE empire of Japan lies to the east of Asia, and consists of four large islands and several smaller ones. It is bounded on the north by the Straits of Perouse and the Straits of Derbrie, on the west by the Sea of Japan and the Straits of Corea, on the south by the Chinese Sea, and on the east by the Pacific Ocean. It is situated between 31° and 45° north latitude, and between 130° and 143°·30′ east longitude. Its length is about 1,000 miles, and its breadth varies from 50 to 200 miles. Its area is 130,000 square miles, and its population is 25,000,000.

Islands and their Provinces.	Chief Towns.	Situation.	Population of Chief Towns.
1. Niphon, 53 Provinces	Jeddo	Gulf of Jeddo.........	1,200,000
	Miako	Yedogawa	700,000
	Osaka	Gulf of Osaka.........	200,000
2. Kin-sin, 4 Provinces........	Naugasaki ..	West Coast............	75,000
3. Sikokf, 9 Provinces.........	Tosa	Seaport	
JAPANESE DEPENDENCIES, CALLED THE GOVERNMENT OF MATSMAI.			
4. Jesso, and some of the adjacent Islands	Matsmai.....	Southern Coast......	60,000

In winter the cold is excessive; and the heat in summer, though tempered by sea breezes, is extreme.

Thunder storms and hurricanes are frequent. The weather is variable, and heavy falls of rain are usual in midsummer. The soil is rather barren, but not unproductive, owing to the moisture of the climate and the industry of the people. Even the sides of the hills are rendered fruitful, as in China; and the whole face of the country, the most rugged districts excepted, presents one universal scene of varied and luxuriant vegetation. The productions of the country are pepper, the tea plant, sugar cane, rice, various esculent roots, the sweet potato, pulse of various kinds, turnips, a kind of cabbage from the seeds of which lamp oil is extracted, indigo, several plants used in dyeing, cotton shrubs, the mulberry, varnish and camphire trees, the vine, the cedar, bamboo reed, both wild and cultivated; and the rhus vermix, which produces a gum-resin, supposed to be the basis of the celebrated black varnish, which derives its name from this country.

In richness of metals, few countries can vie with Japan. Gold is so abundant that, lest its value should diminish, it is prohibited to dig more than a specified quantity. There are also mines of silver, which is here rarer than gold ; abundance of copper, some iron and pit coal, and great quantities of brimstone. There are many warm medicinal springs.

The silk and cotton manufactures rival those of Europe. The porcelain is esteemed superior to that of China ; and the glass is of an excellent description. Many kinds of paper are made from the inner bark of a species of mulberry. Copper, wrought and in bars, precious stones, pearls of exquisite beauty, and lacquered wares, are the principal exports. All trade with Europeans is prohibited, except with the Dutch, who originally purchased the privilege by trampling upon the image of their crucified Lord. The harbours are crowded with vessels, and the inland trade is very considerable.

In no part of Asia are quadrupeds so scarce, as the Japanese, who are great agriculturalists, consider them injurious to their favourite pursuit. Neither sheep nor goats are allowed in the country; but dogs, in some rare instances, are kept, and these only from a superstitious motive. Wolves and foxes are occasionally to be met with. The waters teem with fish, and fowls are abundant.

The government of Japan is an absolute hereditary monarchy, holding the supreme power over a number of absolute hereditary principalities. The government of each province is entrusted to a prince, who is responsible to the Cubo, or secular emperor, for his administration, leaving his family as hostages at the emperor's court. The laws are few, and are rigidly, but impartially administered. They are remarkably severe, most crimes being by them made capital; but the ·sentence cannot be carried into execution without the signature of the Privy Council at Jeddo. Parents and guardians are held responsible for the crimes of those whose education has been confided to their care. The laws are posted up in every village and town, in large letters, in a place surrounded with rails. The army consists of 100,000 infantry and 20,000 cavalry: the navy is insignificant.

The empire of Japan appears to have commenced about 600 years before the Christian era. Until 1,150 A.D., the supreme power was in the hands of the Dairi, an ecclesiastical monarch; but a contest regarding the succession having then arisen, one of the competitors assumed the title and prerogatives of Cubo, or secular emperor, while the other retained the title of Dairi, with the management of religious affairs. At present the Dairi resides in great pomp at Miako; while the Cubo, whose court is at Jeddo, affects to pay him a kind of homage, as if he did but act as his deputy, whereas, in effect, he is the real sovereign.

The language is so peculiar, that it is understood by no other people. They print with a kind of fixed wooden blocks. The schools are numerous; some of those at Miako have each 3,000 or 4,000 scholars. Arithmetic, music, painting, geography, rhetoric, history (especially that of their own country), astronomy, poetry, and domestic economy, make up the ordinary course of study. In Japan, the Chinese is the learned or classic language.

The Japanese are active and dexterous, and of a hardy constitution. Their yellow complexion sometimes inclines to brown, or passes into a pale white. They are chiefly distinguished by a peculiarity in the eyes, which in them are farther from a round shape than in any other people. They have, for the most part, large heads, short necks, and thick black hair. Their moral character is precisely what may be expected from a people involved in all the superstitions and impieties of idolatry. Their manners are, in many respects, diametrically opposite to those of the Europeans—the Turks, in some cases, excepted. Our common drinks are cold—those of the Japanese are hot; we uncover the head out of respect—they the feet; we are fond of white teeth—they of black; we get on horseback on the left side—they on the right. Their houses are of wood, two stories high at most, and are divided in the interior by moveable partitions, sliding in grooves. They take their repast—which is served to each in a basin of porcelain, or on a square salver of japanned ware—sitting on mats or carpets spread on the floor. Their food consists almost entirely of fish, fowl, eggs, and vegetables.

The student of ecclesiastical history must have occasionally remarked that the ground which religion lost in one part of the world was usually gained in another. The remarkable events that happened in the sixteenth century lead directly to that conclusion. The great defection in Europe from the ancient faith of Christ's Church was compensated by the conversion of infidel nations in Asia and America. St. Francis Xavier, one of St. Ignatius's first companions, was the chosen instrument for that great work. This illustrious apostle of the Indies and Japan derived his pedigree from a noble family of Navarre; he was born in the Castle of Xavier, at the foot of the Pyrenees, in 1506; having gone through the lower studies of humanity, in Spain, he went to the University of Paris, where he completed a regular course of philosophy and divinity, and took a master's degree. Under the direction of St. Ignatius he laid the foundation of that eminent sanctity which has raised the admiration of these latter ages. The singular success that accompanied his missionary functions at Venice, Bologna, and Rome, determined the Pope, Paul III., and St. Ignatius to select him as most perfectly qualified for the Indian mission which John III., King of Portugal, was eager to establish. Xavier received his mission from the Pope himself, with the powers of *Nuncius Apostolicus*, and began his journey to Portugal. He embarked at Lisbon on the 7th of April, 1541, in the thirty-fifth year of his age; and on the 6th of May, in the following year, landed at Goa, the capital of the Portuguese settlements in India.

Goa is a considerable town, situated in an island of the same name, originally built by the Moors, and taken from them by the Portuguese in 1510. For the advancement of religion it was erected into a bishop's see, and the viceroy there fixed his residence. Xavier found the city in a most deplorable state of ignorance and corruption. Mahometan Moors and degenerate Christians composed the bulk of its inhabitants. The Portuguese lived more like infidels than Christians, who, having no religious instruction, and being awed by no ecclesiastical authority, lay immersed in a gulf of all those disorderly habits which the thirst of gain, unbridled lust, and revenge, usually create. To reform this second Babylon was the first undertaking of the apostolical Xavier. His labours were incessant; the grace of the Holy Ghost gave unction and effect to his words. Within the course of a few months he had the satisfaction of seeing Goa wholly changed into a new city, both in principle and manners. From Goa the holy missionary turned his eyes toward the coast of the peninsula, which stretches to the south and ends in a point, called Cape Comorin. The country was covered with villages, well peopled, governed by their own chiefs in alliance with the Portuguese. Though little skilled in the Malabar language, Xavier had the address to make himself understood by the idolatrous inhabitants. His engaging manner, his humility, and readiness to help them, drew their respect and attention; they listened, the grace of God infused understanding, they believed, and asked to be baptised. He pursued his course along the coast, and entered the populous kingdom of Travancor, near Cape Comorin. Here the harvest of souls was very abundant; in the space of one month, as he himself informs us, he baptised with his own hand 10,000 souls. In a short time the whole kingdom became Christian; the idolatrous temples were everywhere pulled down, and no less than forty-five churches were erected to the living God. Here the Saint seems to have received the gift of tongues for the first time; here he wrought many miracles— he restored the sick instantaneously to health, and raised four persons from death to life, as is juridically proved. From thence he crossed over to the eastern shore of the peninsula, and went along as far as Meliapor, where St. Thomas the Apostle is said to have suffered martyrdom. The Portuguese gave credit to the tradition, and there built a town, which they named St. Thomas's, in honour of that holy apostle.

Ardent in the pursuit of making the name of Jesus Christ known to the remotest inhabitants of the east, Xavier went on board a vessel at St. Thomas's, sailed across the Gulf of Bengal to Malacca, and from thence to the islands of Molucca, preaching the faith of Christ in every place he came to. In Malacca he met with a native of Japan, whom he converted, and baptized by the name of Paul. Paul accompanied him to the Moluccas, from whence they sailed together to Japan, and landed at Cangoxima, the birth-place of Paul. Japan is, as was stated before, a general name given to a cluster of islands lying in the extremity of the east, opposite to China, between the thirtieth and forty-fifth degrees of northern latitude. The productions of the country in gold, silver, and other precious commodities, afford a lucrative trade to the European merchants. The supreme power of governing is vested, it will be remembered, in an emperor, under whom several petty kings exercise a dependent power. The Japanese are naturally ingenious, and lovers of science, but miserably imposed upon by their hypocritical priests, called Bonzes, who, under the outward show of Pagan rites and sacrifices, delude the people, and provide themselves with every luxury for the indulgence of an idle and voluptuous life. To these idolators, Xavier began to announce the first tidings of Christianity. Though thousands were converted, yet the progress of the gospel amongst them was not equal to his zeal or his expectations. Besides the strong opposition of the Bonzes, he found that the high esteem in which the Chinese were held by the people of Japan, was the next great obstacle to their conversion. When convinced of the Christian truths, and pressed to relinquish their idolatrous worship, many would ask if the Chinese had relinquished theirs. Powerful is the influence which example has at all times over the manners and opinions of men; here it was insuperable; nothing could remove it but the very conversion of the Chinese, whom the Japanese looked up to as to their masters in religious matters. The time for the conversion of China was not yet come, but Xavier resolved to make the attempt, hoping that by gaining one populous empire to the faith of Christ, he should gain another. With that religious view he left Japan, where he had laboured two years and a half, and embarked for China. He landed in the island of Sanciano, near the continent, but was permitted to go no farther. It pleased God there to visit him with his last sickness. A burning fever put an end to his apostolical labours, and opened to him the gate of everlasting rest on the second day of December, 1552. He was a little more than forty-six years of age.

During the ten years which this illustrious Saint employed in the east, for the propagation of the Catholic religion, astonished infidels beheld the miracles and wonders renewed by him, in the name and by the power of his Divine Master, which the first ages of Christianity had witnessed in the apostles. A new world, converted by the preaching and miraculous powers of one man; idolatrous kings bending their necks to the yoke of Christ; the sound of the gospel heard for the first time in the very extremity of the terraqueus globe; and the one, holy, Catholic, Apostolical, and Roman faith established in regions too remote to be noticed by antiquity, are among the glorious trophies of the sixteenth century.*

*It was in 1549, nearly a century after the discovery of Japan by the Portuguese, that St. Francis Xavier landed on its shores. He

B

baptized great numbers, and drew whole provinces to the faith. The powerful kings of Avana, Bungo, and Omura, sent, in 1582, a solemn embassy, declaratory of obedience, to Pope Gregory XIII. Their letters will be found in chapter iv. There were among the Christians in Japan at that time several kings, princes, and bonzes. In 1588, the emperor Cambacundono commenced a sanguinary persecution, which was renewed in four years after, but became most severe under his successor in 1597. At that period, owing to the calumnies of the Dutch merchants, desirous of monopolising the trade of the country, twenty-six martyrs suffered, and all the missionaries, with the exception of twenty-eight, were banished. After the death of the emperor Taik-Sama, the missionaries returned, and in three years converted upwards of 70,000 persons, and erected fifty churches. The persecution was again renewed in 1602; in it and in the subsequent persecutions, both general and partial, it is stated that not less that 1,200,000 Catholics suffered death for their faith. There are still many Christians in Japan. The people of Japan adore idols of the most grotesque shapes: the priests are called Bonzes; all obey the Jaco, or high priest.

CHAPTER III.

IMMEDIATELY after the discovery of Japan, the tidings thereof were speedily conveyed into Europe. An ardent desire to extend the kingdom of God's Church inflamed the hearts, and aroused the energies of men called by God to missionary labours. Their zeal became inflamed, for they felt that they had received a call to labour for the promotion of God's honour and the salvation of newly discovered peoples "*sitting in darkness and the shadow of death.*" Catholic Europe was moved to compassionate the unhappy votaries of pagan rites and pagan ethics ; and whilst the preachers of the word, acting in the spirit of obedience to lawful authority, were severing themselves from all natural ties, and binding themselves to devote all their energies, and even to sacrifice their lives, if necessary, for the extension of religion and the salvation of the human family, there were not wanting generous souls, in every rank in life from the throne to the cottage, who nobly contributed charitable offerings for the promotion of so laudable an enterprise. Christopher Columbus, an illustrious Genoese, amid an array of countless difficulties, commenced a splendid career of gigantic discoveries. The event was the commencement of a new era, and the time was opportune. The whole of the old world was nearly buried under

an accumulated load of vices; the passions were headstrong; insubordination was general and insulting;
the authority of the Church was little heeded; the
"watchmen of Israel" were nodding at their posts;
and heresy and licentiousness were just emerging
from the pit to labour for the general overthrow of all
laws, both human and divine. The base ingratitude
of ancient Christendom was about to receive an awful
chastisement; but, ás the Church would much stand
in need of recruits to fill up the ranks of defection,
God opened a passage to a new world hitherto unheard
of, containing millions of souls, who were to be
brought out of worse than Egyptian darkness " *into
God's admirable light*," and to take that position in the
Church from which the northern nations of Europe
were fast falling away. The success of Columbus
wonderfully stimulated the zeal of men of an enter-
prising genius; it gave an impetus to their labours;
and it very materially tended to develop the latent
powers of the human mind. Navigation became an
important, and, to many, an all-engrossing study;
for, by means of that science, intercommunication
was to take place between all the nations of the earth,
irrespective of distance or dissimilarity of habits. All
obstacles to free intercourse — all impediments to
commercial interchanges—all difficulties in the way
of the evangelisation of the world—were to be gradu-
ally removed by the touch of its magic influence.

The discovery of the new world was both a subject of joy intense and of grief profound. To the man
of the world, whose life is spent in amassing wealth,
and to whom no toil is irksome which is remunerative,
the recent discoveries were a subject of much joy and
thankfulness. To the man whose heart is burning
with love towards God and men, the news that millions were enslaved to their passions, and ignorant of
the law of their God, afforded food for reflection; it

drew forth tears of compassion, and it stimulated missionary zeal. Amidst the awful degeneracy of the times, and the too general corruption of manners, especially amongst the Scandinavian nations, there remained many who had not suffered themselves to be contaminated with the prevailing vices. The Religious Orders and pious congregations, generally speaking, formed a bright exception in their lives to the every day example of those degenerate times. The men of the age were greatly corrupted, but not wholly so. Some few remained faithful. For, though Europe in many places was wavering in her faith, and many of her cities were sinks of moral turpitude; though many of her monarchs were professional liber-tines and oppressors of the Church, and too many of her churchmen were morally corrupt or criminally apathetic, yet it contained many sound elements of faith, especially amongst those who, by vow, had renounced all for Christ. The Religious Orders were almost exclusively possessed of the missions in heretical and heathen countries; and they joyfully went forth to sow the gospel seed amongst the Gentiles and all barbarous nations. They well remembered that the blood of an incarnate Saviour had been lovingly and profusely shed on Calvary's rugged top, not for Christians *only*, but for Jews, Pagans, and all Barbarians; in a word, for all mankind, without a single exception. They remembered, too, the words of the Redeemer: "*And other sheep I have, that are not of this fold : them also I must bring, and they shall hear my voice, and there shall be one fold and one shepherd.*"— (St. John x. 16.) The Society of Jesus, as was noticed in the preceding chapter, had just sprung up, and had supplied the Church militant with a fresh army of fervent and zealous missionaries; men of indomitable energy, possessing talents of the highest order, and whose lives were not only blameless, but distinguished for sanctity in an eminent degree. The great Orders of St. Francis of Assisium and of St. Dominic, which had been so rapidly spread over the surface of the whole earth, and which from the very commencement had sent zealous missionaries into all parts of the known world, had endured the severest persecutions whilst carrying on their labour of love; thousands of their children had suffered martyrdom in Morocco, in Turkey, in various other parts of Africa and of Asia, and also in America, shortly after the period of its discovery. The powerful help of the Society of Jesus, just brought into being by a special providence, came very opportunely to continue, but upon a more gigantic scale, perhaps, the great missionary work of conversion amongst the Gentiles. St. Francis Xavier, the Apostle of the Indies, the renowned Thaumaturgus of the sixteenth century, as stated in chapter ii., first undertook to evangelise the Japanese, in the year 1549.

It may be well to again notice here how wonderful were the ways of divine providence at a time when Europe was generally growing cold in faith, and when in many countries a great relaxation of morals amongst both clergy and people had taken place. Those evils were the fatal harbingers of that awful revolution of which Luther was the unhappy author, in Saxony. Wretched man! You were the first to stir up, and, as it were, to collect in one all the evil elements and unruly passions which had been working in European society for some years previously. It is true that zealous voices were heard here and there, and even wonderful prodigies were performed by some special servants of God to awaken the people; but all attempts to effect a beneficial change, if they were not altogether vain, at least proved unavailing to produce that general "*revival*" which it was the aim of so many extraordinary preachers and zealous pontiffs, and the special object of the holy founders of Religious Orders, to effect. St. Paul first preached to his countrymen, the Jews; but when he found them hardened in heart, and deaf to the voice of God calling them in loving mercy to aggregate themselves to his holy Church— when he found them wilfully unfitted and unprepared to receive the glad tidings of salvation, he turned his attention to the heathens, or Gentiles.

This grand work was carried on in every age since the establishment of Christianity. And when the old world had forgotten its first love and had grown wanton, when it began to revolt from its obedience and to walk after its own lusts, then God discovered new worlds and innumerable peoples till then unheard of, to whom the glad tidings of the gospel were carried as it were on the wings of the wind; the seeds of religious truth were sown broadcast amongst the Indians, Americans, and Japanese; and there produced the wonderful fecundity predicted by our Lord Jesus Christ, who had commissioned his apostles and their disciples to preach to all the nations of the earth, giving them a solemn guarantee that "*the gates of hell shall not prevail against*" his chaste spouse, the Catholic Church.

The faith was preached in Japan for 40 years by St. Francis Xavier and other holy and zealous missionaries, and more than 2,000,000 of the Japanese. had received the law of Christ in that short period of time. Churches, chapels, and oratories were built, and schools were opened in quick succession, appearing one after the other in the same ratio as a clear idea of Christianity had informed their minds, and gained for the truth of its dogmas the full assent of their wills. Morals, as a necessary result, were soon expurgated, and society generally was regenerated under the holy impulse and influence of the Holy Ghost. More labourers were soon needed, and a plentiful supply was speedily

procured. Everything promised an abundant harvest
of souls, when the devil, resorting to his old wiles,
soon suggested plans for the extirpation of Christianity from the land. Yes; this great success of
Christianity in Japan excited the fury of hell; and,
as violence and persecution were always the means
employed to eradicate religion, so, in this instance,
when persuasion was tried, and failed, persecution of
the most sanguinary description was resorted to, that
at one fell swoop every vestige of it might be eradicated
from the land.

We may here observe that the gospel truths are
so simple, and clear, and demonstrable, the enemies
of Christianity have never tried conviction or argu-
ment to refute them; for if they have pretended to
do so, it was only for a very brief period. They soon
found the ground slipping from under them, and
disappointment engendered revenge. Persecution
then arose—cruelty was used as the easiest mode of
extermination, and became a weapon in the hands of
the wicked for counteracting the beneficent designs
of Christ, for accomplishing the great work of man's
redemption. Tertullian has said, "That truth and
the hatred of it commenced together." Hence we
find persecution from the Jews, from the Pagan
Roman emperors, from heretical and schismatical
·princes and governors, from false brethren, from
treacherous foes; in a word, from all who have preferred the idolatry of the passions to the pure worship of God, who through love for man assumed his
nature and died for his ransom. This common way
of acting against Christianity was also applied to
Japan. When the persecution first broke out, Japan
was governed by the tyrannical and licentious Taiko-
Sama, a monster of depravity, who continually
indulged his passions, among which his libidinous
propensities were the strongest. This horrible man

was so wicked that he kept more than 300 concubines to gratify his lusts. He sent his agents over
all the country to collect the most beautiful damsels
for the vile gratification of his sensual desires; but
all the Christian daughters resisted him, and not one
of them could be induced to become a court lady of
this impious tyrant. This refusal of the Christian
daughters was the first pretext for the foul persecution that deluged Japan with blood, and paved the
way for the nearly utter ruin of Catholicity. The
bonzes, or Japanese idolatrous priests, seeing with
jealousy and anger the pure morals of the Christian
people (which were a constant condemnation of their
own lasciviousness), their fraternity, their unity, and
their numbers continuously increasing, used every
exertion with Taiko-Sama to destroy and ruin the
missionaries. The ambition of Taiko-Sama was so
great that he wished to be adored as a god by all his
subjects—an honour which, of course, the Christians
were obliged to unanimously refuse to give him. A
certain Tacuinus, an impious man, and, like his
master and the bonzes, addicted to all the turpitude
of Pagan superstition, took hold of the opportunity
of their refusal to allure the Christians into rebellion
against, and transgression of, the laws of the country.
Taiko-Sama, inflamed by furious passions, and glad
to have found a good pretext to colour his cruelty in
the eyes of his subjects, ordered all the churches and
chapels dedicated to Christian worship to be destroyed, and all the crosses to be pulled down ; and
he proscribed and banished all the missionaries. No
violence, however great, no persecution, however
long continued, can ever eradicate the divine seed of
Christianity when firmly implanted in the hearts of
men. Some missionaries remained hidden, and, under
various disguises, continued to attend to the wants
of the Catholic people ; giving to them all the com-

forts of religion — being deprived of every other blessing. Thus, working in secret, the zealous missionaries upheld the work of God; but by degrees the number of labourers in the vineyard diminished, and in a very few years only a small number of missionaries remained in Japan. During the fearful persecution of the Christians, under Taiko-Sama, it is reported that 200,000 suffered martyrdom. This number seems incredible, but we must bear in mind that, by the greatness of their number, they caused much uneasiness to Taiko-Sama; and thus it is not improbable that at that time there were nearly 2,000,000 of native Christians. On considering the fury with which they were maltreated—no women, no children being spared, the number of 200,000 martyrs is not an improbable calculation. However, Taiko-Sama and his minions were foiled in their attempts; their designs were not wholly successful. To use the beautiful language of Tertullian: "*Sanguis martyrum semen Christianorum*"— "*The blood of the martyrs is the seed of Christians.*" Yes; the blood of the martyrs was the seed which grew, bearing abundant fruit afterwards—as we shall see in the succeeding chapters—until it was again crushed; but it is destined to revive at the time appointed by divine providence.

CHAPTER IV.

To spend one's life in missionary labours amongst
barbarous peoples, amidst appalling privations, and
in hourly expectation of meeting with cruel tortures
or an ignominious death, and all this from a sincere
desire to promote God's honour and man's salvation,
is the highest act of homage a man is capable of pay-
ing his Creator; it is, too, the surest test of his fulfilling the double law of "*loving God above all things,
and his neighbour as himself.*" The Eternal Wisdom,
who, compassionating our fallen nature, vouchsafed
"*to stoop down to earth to raise up man to heaven,*" has
positively declared that "*greater love than this no man
hath, that a man lay down his life for his friends*"—
(St. John, xv. 13). In establishing His church, He
not only foresaw, but he also predicted, that the
world and the powers of darkness would be always
combined together for her overthrow. It is true that
His veracity stands pledged for her perpetual existence; but then He promised to His disciples, as the
reward of their labours here in His service, contradictions, privations, contempt, imprisonment, and a cruel
death. To give proof to the whole world that the
holy Catholic Church, is the work of His love and
omnipotence, He has, in every age of her being,

raised up extraordinary men, wholly devoid of self,
full of charity, and burning with an ardent zeal to
change the face of the earth, to purify it from moral
guilt, and to reconcile men to God. It was by such
men that the world was converted. It was by such
men that true liberty and real civilisation were first
made known to the nations. If we commence with
the glorious deacon and proto-martyr of the Christian Church, St. Stephen, and end with the last hero,
who shed his blood in Cochin China for the sake of
Jesus Christ, and for the conversion of the heathens,
what a glorious army of Christian worthies we behold?
What a noble subject of reflection to the mind of the
Christian philosopher is presented in the lives, labours,
and sufferings of that countless host, whom God raised
up in every age to combat with hell, and to vindicate
the ways of His Providence! These men were real
reformers, not like the spurious ones, who trace their
pedigree from Simon Magus, and have been labouring
with the prince of darkness by an admixture of Christian truths and philosophical speculations, to subvert
true religion, and to lead men from obedience and
faith into the by-ways of insubordination and error.
Faith is *one*, and loyalty is *indispensable ;* and the salvation of men is of such paramount importance, that
it required the death of a Man-God to effect its accomplishment. Pride is the bane of virtue and religion,
and humility is the antidote. Pride has always led
to heresy and schism—to the relaxation of Christian
morals, and to the local displacement of the foundations of the Catholic religion. Humility has subdued
the pride of the intellect and the pride of the heart;
consolidated the foundations of faith, extended its
influence, propagated its dogmas, brought hope to
the wanderer, certainty to the doubting, grace to the
sinner, felicity to the world, and courage to the martyr.
What a long and illustrious list of *real* reformers are

found in the annals of religion ? In every age, either the absence of religious persecution, or the intrigues of State-craft, have superinduced a relaxation of morals, the consequences of which have always been deplorable. For not only have individuals been punished for their delinquency, but whole nations have been visited by summary chastisements ; and rebellion against religion has been very frequently punished by the deprivation of liberty, and by the loss of worldly greatness; or by the accumulation of the means fitted for the gratification of ambition, or the indulgence of libidinous propensities, two of the greatest evils which God in His anger permits nations to fall into, for the punishment of their perfidy. Read the lives of such men as SS. Benedict, Francis, Dominic, John of Matha, Peter Nolasco, Bruno, Bernard, Ignatius of Loyola, B. Paul of the Cross, &c. How pure their lives ! how staunch their loyalty ! how multitudinous their labours ! how constant their zeal ! how persevering their movements ! how grand their object ! how heroic their sacrifices ! how glorious their ends ! They still live in their disciples ; the work goes on, and it prospers, for God watches over it. He it was who formed the mind that conceived it, and furnished the energy by which it was accomplished. Behold the fruits, in every age and clime. Roman power was too weak to crush it. Jewish perfidy and Pagan corruption could not impede its onward march. Christian degeneracy might retard, but could not wholly stop it; and even the gates of hell were unable to effect its ruin. Let the nations of the earth, brought by missionary zeal within the pale of the " *one sheepfold of the one Shepherd,*" recount the blessings which were carried to them by those renowned reformers whom God had specially selected for the renovation of the world ; for their labours spread true civilisation cotemporaneously with true

·religion; and it is owing to their burning zeal, fortified by God's blessing, that the world has not wholly degenerated and become a very Pandemonium. Let us return to the Japanese. So great was the success of Xavier; so numerous were the conversions which, notwithstanding the many obstacles that beset his path, he effected in the short compass of thirty months, and so zealous were his successors in carrying on the glorious work, that we find royal embassies were sent to Rome, to Pope Gregory XIII., carrying with them letters breathing fullness of faith and submission.

The following letters are replete with interest, and the sincere Christian will arise from their perusal with a heart full of love and gratitude. The first is from the King of Bungo to Pope Gregory XIII. The inscription of the letter is—

" To the Adorable who holds on earth the place of the King of Heaven, to the great and very holy Pope."

The king says :—

" Having invoked, with great humility, the assistance of the Sovereign God, I humbly write to your Holiness. The Lord who governs heaven and earth, and whose empire is above the sun, the moon, and the stars, who commanded the light to shine in darkness, comes to open in a peculiar manner to our people the treasures of His mercy. He vouchsafed, more than thirty years ago, to send the missionaries into this kingdom; and through them my heart, by the goodness of God, has received part in their salutary and divine doctrine. I acknowledge that this great benefit, and so many others, have not reached me except owing to your prayers and merits, O Holy Father of all Christians. If I were not prevented by the burden of continual wars—by the weight of old age and all its infirmities—I should have gone myself to visit the holy places, and render to you the obedience which I owe to you, and would have put my head under thy feet after having kissed them reverently ; and I should also go to receive the blessing from your holy hands.

" Unable to go myself, I wished to send to you the son of my sister, Prince Jerome, son also of the King of Fiunga; but being absent, and the Visitor being anxious to depart, I send you his cousin, the Prince Mancio. I shall feel exceedingly obliged if your Holiness will continue to help and assist me. I have received with great joy the relics which your Holiness has sent me, and have placed them with great respect on my head. I feel more thankful to your Holiness than my words can express. I shall not be longer, for the Father Visitor will tell you more about me, my personal concerns, and the concerns of my kingdom. Addressing this letter, with great respect and veneration, to your Holiness, whom I honour in truth and sincerity, this 11th day of January, A.D. 1582, I kiss the feet of your Beatitude.

"FRANCIS, KING OF BUNGO."

The second letter is from Bartholomew, Prince of Omura. It has the following inscription :—

"That this letter be given to the great and holy Lord whom I honour, as holding the place of God on earth."

The Prince writes as follows :—

" With the grace of God, I humbly present these letters to your Holiness. It is now two years since, during Lent, in which special mention is made of the passion of our Lord Jesus Christ— my family being enveloped in the horrors of war, all my affairs upset, and myself buried in the darkness of Paganism—the Father of mercies vouchsafed to show me the light of His truth, and the right way to arrive to salvation, through the care of the true Visitor and other missionaries, preachers of the Word of God, who have greatly assisted me, and brought over me and mine the dew of divine grace by baptism, for which I constantly give thanks to the King of Heaven. And because your Holiness governs the whole of Christianity, I anxiously desired to visit you, and to give to you humble obedience, prostrated on the ground; and after having kissed your blessed feet, place the same holy feet upon my head. But being retained in my kingdom by several affairs, I send you, with the Father Visitor, Prince Michael, my cousin, that he may fulfil for me this filial duty. And your holiness, whom I honour with the great respect of an humble and sincere heart, will know my sentiments. For this reason I shall not be long. The 8th of January, A.D. 1582."

He concludes by saying that he " prostrates himself at the feet of the Holy Father."

The third letter is also from the Prince of Omura, who had lost the greatest part of his estates for having embraced the Christian religion. • It bears the following inscription :—

*" The hands lifted up to heaven offer this letter with veneration to our
very holy Pope, who holds the place of God on earth."*

The Prince thus addresses Gregory XIII.:—

"I fear to be too bold and too free, judging that it would
be more just for me to cross the seas to visit your Holiness, who
holds the place of God on earth, and to place on my head your
holy feet, having respectfully kissed them ; but various reasons
preventing me from doing so, and the Visitor of the holy missionaries being ready to leave, having worthily visited all these
distant countries, I have profited by this favourable opportunity
to send with him to your Holiness the son of my brother, the
Prince Michael, who, though young and unfit for so important a mission, will be graciously admitted to kiss your feet ; for
which benefit I shall be infinitely obliged to your Holiness, whom
I supplicate and humbly entreat to remember me, and to be so
kind as to favour me and all the Christian Japanese, which is all
I desire. Your Holiness will learn the rest from the Visitor and
the Prince Michael.

"I wrote this on the 27th of January, 1582.

"I, Bartholomew, throw myself on the ground, humbled
under thy holy feet."

How edifying are these letters ! how consoling !
how full of faith and love ! how consolatory to the
heart of the learned and venerated Pontiff must have
been their contents ! Europe was convulsed by religious controversy and civil commotion to which it
gave birth. Religious novelties had fascinated the
minds and drawn the hearts of those who wished to
substitute licence for obedience, and human philosophy for divine revelation. Wars, seditions, heresy,
and schism were rapidly drawing the northern nations
into the vortex of infidelity and licentiousness. The
Church was losing, or had lost, some of her finest
provinces at the bidding, or through the threats, of a
rebellious monk and a licentious king. Sanguinary
feuds, ruthless sacrilege, monastic demolition, and the
robbery of the poor, were the order of the day. The
whole of western Christendom became the battle-
field of strife, and crimes were openly committed by

man against man, in the name of religion, which could only have been perpetrated by men inspired by the Prince of Darkness. The ruin of innumerable souls, the havoc inflicted upon religion, the injuries sustained by society, of which religion is the mainstay, must have deeply wounded the loving hearts of all the true disciples of the Redeemer, and much more his who is Christ's Vicegerent, and who stands to us in the place of God. But in the midst of all those tumults, and scandals, and revolts, how refreshing to the soul of Gregory XIII. must have been the presence of the Japanese Ambassadors, bearing with them such glorious tokens of homage and affection. A new world brought to light, and her people already in great numbers filling those places in the Church from which so many of the people of northern Europe had departed, must, indeed, have been the work of God. Grand must have been the spectacle, and the joy which it excited must have been ineffable. On that day the angelic choir must have attuned their harps and have chanted their psalmody; the very vaults of heaven must have vibrated, when, taking up again the chorus of Bethlehem, they sang, with loud and sonorous voices, "*Gloria in altissimis Deo, et in terra pax hominibus bonæ voluntatis.*"

C

CHAPTER V.

HAVING given, in the preceding chapters, an outline of Japan, and of the labours of St. Francis Xavier, we must now draw nearer to our object. Our readers being now familiar with the scene, or theatre, where the children of St. Francis of Assisium are to labour and gain the immortal crown. God seems to work slowly, yet He reaches the end surely. He had decreed that Japan should receive the light of faith; that the humble children of St. Francis should be the most zealous missionaries in Japan; but He does not send them all at once, but slowly and by the concurrence of various circumstances. He brings them at last into the field which He intended for them. It is necessary that we follow providence in its ways, and accompany our heroes to their first expedition to the Philippine Islands, so called because they were discovered under Philip II. of Spain.

In the kingdom of Peru there lived a very rich man, who, being moved by the grace of God, and stimulated by the wonderful example of St. Francis, sold all his goods and became a lay brother; his name was Anthony. He soon made extraordinary progress in virtue and perfection. He prayed constantly for the conversion of the inhabitants of the Philippine Islands, then just discovered. By a special revelation from God, he knew that he was to be the first instrument to bring to those forlorn islanders the glad tidings of the gospel of Christ. He asks permission to go, but it is refused. He prays to God again and again, and he iterates his solicitation for permission, but again his superiors absolutely refuse. At length, by dint of importunity, he obtains leave to go to Spain to consult his higher superiors about his intended mission. Whilst on his voyage to Europe, he fell into the hands of French pirates, who treated him cruelly and threw him overboard; but God preserved him, and he landed safe at Seville. In Spain he solicited the superiors of the Order, but his request is refused on the plea that he was not fitted for such a mission. But he never tired of soliciting, and ultimately Francis Gusman gave him permission to go over with seventeen others. They embarked in 1577, but seven died on the passage, the others landed safely in Mexico, and sailed from a town called Acapulco to the Philippine Islands, where the Viceroy received them with great affection, as he had frequently asked the Franciscan Fathers to evangelise the idolators.

Brother Anthony returned to Spain to bring other missionaries. He again fell into the hands of French pirates, who, having treated him most cruelly, tied him to the mast and made preparations for shooting him. But God again delivered his servant, by moving the barbarians to compassion. The other fathers who remained in the Philippine Islands, settled down at Manilla, and having studied the language, in a short time they preached with great zeal. The principal man of the party was Peter Alphoro, who, in 1579, went over to China, founded a Convent at Macoa, then set out for Goa, from which place he sailed to

Malacca, but was shipwrecked and drowned, with all his companions and others. Whilst dying himself in the sea, he preached to the others, and gave them absolution of their sins. His body, resplendent with glory, was discovered in a praying attitude.

Brother Anthony obtained from Pope Gregory XIII. special powers to select as many missionaries from the Franciscan body as he might deem requisite. He chose forty. The Papal *Nuntius Apostolicus*, who was called Sega, gave them a splendid banner, wrought in gold, representing the blessed Virgin standing, having on one side St. Francis of Assisium, and on the other St. Anthony of Padua. After a Pontifical High Mass, he gave to the forty the banner, saying, with tears:—" *Receive this Banner of the Cross, to conquer the enemies of our Faith.*" He appointed Father Michael of Talavere to be their superior : a man of transcendant abilities, a doctor of divinity in the University of Alcala. Amongst the number of those missionaries then sent out with Brother Anthony, were the principal heroes of our present historical epitome.

The forty members thus chosen, were all of the most excellent dispositions; clever in theology, and eminent in virtues. God, by a miracle, showed how much good would arise from this mission. There appeared above the Church, in which they were assembled, a large flaming cross; and two Brothers of eminent sanctity obtained a revelation that it was from those apostolical men the light of faith should spring forth to the Indians, and many other barbarous nations.

Let us now give a brief sketch of the lives of the principal martyrs, who were amongst the forty holy men who went out from Spain to the Philippine Islands, and from thence to Japan.

1. Petrus Baptista, born in the village of San Estevan, in the diocese of Avila, in Spain. He studied at the Franciscan School of Salamanca. He took the Habit and was professed at Arenas. He became master of philosophy and divinity; was several times guardian, or superior, of the convent; he governed his brethren with great prudence, and led them in the way of perfection. Whilst guardian at Merida, he was sent to the Philippine Islands. As soon as he became a missionary, he spent the night in prayer, and the day in apostolic labours; teaching, preaching, and visiting the hospitals. He always said mass very early in the morning, and treated his body with great severity; using every day the discipline to blood. He retired, from time to time, into a private convent, to give rest to his soul, and to work exclusively for his own perfection. He was elected Bishop of Camerines, but he refused the dignity. He was, however, compelled to accept the mitre, but, before he could be consecrated, he was sent as ambassador to Japan, and obtained there the crown of martyrdom.

2. Martinus de Aguirre was born at Fergora, in Biscay, in Spain. He was professor of divinity in the convent at Madrid, when God inflamed his heart with zeal for becoming a missionary in Japan. He prayed to the Blessed Virgin to know the will of God in his regard. He fasted and performed the most rigorous penances, to ascertain his vocation. One night he heard a secret voice whispering in his soul, that God had chosen him to be one of the pillars of the church in Japan. He possessed nothing except one habit and his breviary. He never ate meat or fish, but only vegetables and bread, and drank only water. He always went barefooted, slept little, passed the greatest part of the night in prayer, and when overwhelmed with sleep, he took a bloody discipline, to keep himself awake. By those extraordinary

penances he preserved his purity without the least blemish. His compassion for the poor was so great, that when he met lepers he fell on his knees and kissed their wounds. He practised, during six years, all those virtues, and when he went out to the Philippine Islands, and afterwards to Japan, he only added fresh penances, and redoubled his austerities, fastings, and prayers, and by such means he made himself worthy of the crown of martyrdom.

3. Franciscus Blanco was born at Monterey, in Gallicia, in Spain. He received the Seraphical Habit in the Province of St. James; and, whilst yet young, he went over to the Philippine Islands, and then to Japan. He had a very singular devotion to the Blessed Virgin, and he fasted most severely on all Saturdays. He was very attentive and punctual in his devotions, and gave long hours to high contemplation. · He preserved purity undefiled until his last breath, and his whole appearance inspired love for the holy virtue of chastity. He was accustomed to take the discipline three times every night; he never spoke a useless word, but, in all his occupations, he was constantly engaged with God As soon as he was ordained Priest he went out to Japan, where he was of the greatest utility, since he knew well the Japanese language. He was the first who preached and heard confessions in the Japanese tongue. He showed extraordinary zeal in relieving not only the miseries of the soul, but even those of the body. He served the lepers with great attention and kindness, and constantly showed himself their father and physician. He never shrank from the greatest sacrifices, when he could make himself useful to the unfortunate and the miserable.

4. Philippus de Jesu was born in Mexico. He spent his youthful years in luxury and pleasure. His pious parents not being able to bring him to a

regular and a steady life, began to look upon him with great aversion and coldness. This touched him to the quick, and caused him to begin to reflect more seriously; and, listening to the sweet inspirations of grace, he entered the severe Order of St. Francis. But, being yet weak in virtue and ignorant of the snares of the devil, he left the noviceship and returned to his former mode of life. This inconstancy on his part very much displeased his parents, who rejected him altogether, and would no longer tolerate him in their presence. They sent him to China to learn the business of a merchant. God again looked favourably upon him, moved his heart, which was tortured by severe remorse because he had left the happy state of the religious life, and found himself separated, through his own fault, from all who were dear to his affections, and in the midst of the greatest dangers of soul and body. Those serious reflections had so much influence over him that he resolved to spare no trouble to gain re-admission into the Order, and to answer thoroughly the inspirations of the Holy Ghost. He arrived at Manilla, put all his affairs in good order, and, for the second time, asked for the penitential Habit, which he was permitted to receive. He was very fervent during his noviceship, and at the end of a year, he made his solemn profession. This event caused extraordinary joy to his parents, who were noble and rich, and had great influence in the world. They used their utmost exertions to induce the Superior General Commissary to grant him permission to go over to his parents, that they might enjoy the happiness of seeing their son in the holy habit of the Seraphical Order. The Commissary being unable to resist the force of the importunity, hesitated no longer, he yielded to their pressing and oft-repeated solicitations, and gave leave to Philip de Las Casas (for that was his name before he entered upon the religious life) to go over and give his family the satisfaction they desired. He went on board of a Spanish vessel, but met with a furious gale, which ended in a hurricane; the vessel was carried by the waves into one of the Japanese harbours, and at that time a sanguinary persecution was raging in Japan against the professors of Christianity. When Philip heard of the sufferings of his brethren, he joined himself gladly to them, and obtained the unexpected crown of martyrdom, for which great blessing he gave great and hearty thanks to God, and died with much cheerfulness.

5. Gonsalvus Garcia was born at Becaim, in the East Indies. He was a merchant, and carried on business very extensively. He had traded for many years with the Japanese. He frequently sailed to Manilla, where he always paid a visit to to the Franciscans, for whom he felt a very great affection. On a certain day, quite suddenly, he felt within himself a great and almost irresistible impulse to become a Franciscan Friar, and to take care of his soul. Gonsalvus was not deaf to this holy inspiration, but settled at once all his affairs, took the Habit, persevered in the noviceship with great fervour, withstood with extraordinary firmness the temptations and assaults of the devil, and at length made his solemn profession. By his zeal and fervour he obtained from God the grace of receiving the immortal crown of heavenly treasures, in that very land in which he had gained so much temporal profit. He was the inseparable companion of Petrus Baptista, and acted as interpreter. He ardently loved God, and was always most zealous in labouring to gain souls to Christ. Gonsalvus Garcia had, when yet in the Philippine Islands, a great affection for the Japanese. He was always ready to assist them, more especially those amongst them

who were miserable; he served them with the greatest
charity, and gave them salutary admonitions. As he
well knew their language, the Japanese liked him, and
the native Christians frequently used to get him to act
as their interpreter when they were engaged in making
their confessions. The Emperor of Japan loved this
brother with great affection, because he had known
him as a merchant; and his esteem for the brother
greatly increased when he heard that he had abandoned all earthly goods for the love of Jesus, his divine
Master, and in the hope of a better life. The Emperor
praised this generous conduct, but could not well
understand how the Christians could be so detached
from all worldly goods, and renounce all for God.
He admired, but the grace of God was wanting; or
rather, he was deaf to its sweet invitations.

6. Franciscus of St. Michael was born at Parilla,
near Valladolid, in Spain, where he took the Habit
and lived in great holiness, observing his rule most
strictly. He was a great lover of holy poverty. He
never would wear a new Habit, and never used any
sandals, but always went quite barefoot. He scourged
his mortified body with sanguinary disciplines. He
fasted all the Lent, in the same manner as our Holy
Father St. Francis used to fast, and never took any
collation in the evening. He attained, in an eminent
degree, the practice of contemplative prayer, and he
kept a constant silence, lest he might lose this great
gift by dissipation and too great familiarity. He
never looked at any woman, but turned his eyes
away; for he had experienced much severe temptation,
having once in early life been grievously tormented
from an imprudent, though innocent glance. His
greatest pleasure was to kneel before the Tabernacle,
and there silently and lovingly adore the Blessed
Sacrament. He was frequently rapt in ecstasies,
when he contemplated the love of our Lord Jesus

Christ, in the Blessed Eucharist. He invoked the
Immaculate Mary, and loved her as his own dear
mother and advocate, and he always looked upon her
with the greatest confidence for help in the greatest
troubles of both soul and body. He had also a great
affection for the poor suffering members of Christ's
mystical body ; he never dismissed them without
giving them something : he even subtracted from his
own scanty meal to supply their need. He served
the incurables in the hospitals, and was always
cheerful in countenance. But, above all his other
virtues appeared his zeal for the conversion of the
Japanese. Every day he said the rosary for that
purpose, that he might obtain through the powerful
intercession of the Blessed Virgin this great favour.
He was gifted with eloquence in a supereminent
degree, and it rose to sublimity when the theme of
his discourse was the conversion of the natives of
Japan. He was accustomed to say that no wind was
so agreeable to him as the one which blew towards
Japan. He was the beloved companion of Petrus
Baptista, in his embassy to Japan. He was also
favoured with the gifts of miracles. On a certain
day he was called to attend upon an Indian woman
who had lost the use of speech. The holy Brother
made the sign of the cross over her mouth, and she
began to speak, asking to be baptised and to be
received into the Catholic Church. On another
occasion an Indian had been bitten by a serpent,
which reptile is very venomous in those countries,
Brother Francis made the sign of the cross, and the
unfortunate Indian was instantaneously cured. He
possessed a very extraordinary memory, for whatever
he heard, or read, he retained wholly, and that was
the reason why he learned so soon and so well the
difficult Japanese language. By his untiring zeal to
implant in their minds and hearts the principles of

the Christian Religion, he converted an immense number of the people of Japan. One day at Macoa, he was busily engaged in decorating the Sepulchre, or the place in the chapel in which the Blessed Sacrament is kept on Maunday Thursday ; the Japanese stared admiringly, but could not understand what he was about. On Holy Thursday, when all the decorations were well finished, and the place was adorned with many lights, he went near the place, took off his upper clothes, and ordered a Japanese to bind him to a pillar and scourge him till his whole back was one large wound, and the blood flowed in streams upon the ground. When this was done he took a crucifix into his hands, and with a heart burning with divine love he fervently supplicated God, that He in His great mercy would hasten the conversion of the Japanese. By these and such like devotions and practices, he endeavoured to make Pagans understand what our dear and loving Lord Jesus Christ had suffered for the love of us, and for our salvation. He died the death of a martyr.

CHAPTER VI.

THE intrigues of the Dutch, who aimed at the commercial monopoly of the trade of Japan, caused the great disturbances which arose in that empire. They excited the Japanese against the Portuguese and Spaniards, with the hope that by dividing them amongst themselves, they (the Dutch) might more easily obtain their object. They also excited the religious and temporal elements of Japan against each other, and they shrank from no meanness or baseness in order to attain their end. History abundantly informs us of their conduct in later years. However, they failed at that time. The powerful, ingenious, though rude and savage, Taiko-Sama,* who, from the humblest position, raised himself to the rank of general, was naturally clever and talented. He took advantage of every opportunity to extend his influence, in all the troubles in which Japan was then involved. At last he saw a way was opened for him, and, taking hold of the throne, he declared himself emperor. He several times engaged in war, and with success. Japan was then divided into a great number of principalities, or petty states, and was governed by no fewer than

---

* Taiko-Sama means Most Exalted and Sovereign Lord.

seventy kings. But Taiko reduced nearly all of them, and obliged the others to recognise his supremacy. Taiko, finding himself so successful, became so elated with pride that he resolved to conquer the whole world. He sent Ferranda, a common man, to the Philippine Islands, with orders to announce to the Governor the great power of Taiko-Sama, who had resolved to conquer by force those who should resist his amicable offers. Ferranda, therefore, had received a commission to ask the Governor of the Islands to endeavour to induce Philip II., King of Spain, to recognise the supremacy of Taiko-Sama if he wished not to be driven from his dominions. The Governor was greatly troubled at hearing this strange news, and the citizens of Manilla were thrown into great consternation, for every one feared or expected treachery. But as the affair appeared of such mighty consequence, the Governor resolved to send Father Cobos, with precious gifts, to Taiko-Sama; and he also gave him letters for the emperor, in which it was represented that he and the leading men under him doubted the seriousness of the embassy, on account of the low rank of the ambassador. Father Cobos was received with great honour by the emperor, in 1592, and he showed so much satisfaction in seeing him, that he sent immediately another ambassador of higher rank to the Governor of the Philippine Islands, with letters containing instructions for making a lasting peace. Father Cobos, who returned with his suite by the way of Harmanos, was cruelly murdered, with all his companions, by the savage inhabitants of that island, who, in hope of finding great treasures in their possession, stripped them of everything. But as the ministers of religion had no temporal advantage in view, but were only solicitous for the spiritual good and the immortal salvation of all the Pagans, they practised strict poverty, without preserving any thing. The savages were much disap-

pointed at finding no riches, and, maddened by fury
and anger, they put them all to death. Father Cobos
was the bearer of very important letters, as was afterwards ascertained, but his death caused those letters
to be lost; and the citizens of Manilla, not being
aware of the death of Father Cobos, were more
suspicious on the arrival of the second embassy, and
principally because the whole city had been swarming,
during the last few days, with Japanese, who, under
various pretexts, had obtained a landing. However,
their fear and anxiety soon vanished when the new
ambassador produced some letters from Father Cobos,
who had very prudently with much forethought, given
him some documents to show his authority in case he
should arrive before the Father at Manilla. Nevertheless, the new ambassador had not proofs in his
possession that sufficient powers had been delegated
to him (for these had been more fully committed and
explained to Father Cobos), to conclude a treaty of
peace and commerce; he was thus left unable to
attain the object of his mission. He remained a long
time at Manilla, and during his stay he frequently
visited the Franciscan Fathers in their convent; in
which place he constantly met a great number of
Japanese, who were very familiar and friendly with
the Fathers, but more especially with Brother Gonsalvus, who spoke their own language, and whom
they had known as a merchant in Japan. The
ambassador frequently showed to the good brother
letters that had been written by several persons, who
were desirous to see the Franciscan Friars settled in
Japan. He declared, too, that the emperor was very
favourable to their going thither. Taiko-Sama had
some good qualities, and it is very probable that if he
had been able to act for himself, and on his own
account—if he had not listened to ill advice, or permitted himself to be influenced by the corrupt and

immoral Bonzes and other superstitious idolators, who, knowing well the ambition of Taiko, made use of it to frighten him against favouring the Christians, who they falsely and calumniously stated, were conspiring against the emperor, and whose throne was to be, sooner or later, subverted by them. By the constant repetition of those false accusations, they slowly poisoned his mind; nevertheless, Taiko listened, now and then, to the higher and nobler suggestions of his heart, and showed himself more favourably disposed to the Christians. Some historians pretend that he was devoid of every gentle. and humane feeling; and that if, by times, he displayed a little sympathy in his dealings towards the Christians, he merely acted from political motives; that, being too much engaged in the wars that were being continually carried on between the petty princes of the nation and himself, and, having noticed very frequently the dissatisfaction of the subdued tribes, he could not conveniently execute the decree for the extirpation of the Catholic faith; that, moreover, he was anxious to bring about the concluding of a treaty favourable to his people in a commercial point of view, with the Christian King of Spain; and, therefore, that for all these reasons (say the historians), he thought it more prudent to temporise and show himself favourable to the Christians; especially as the ambassadors, who had been sent to Rome some months previously by the converted princes, were at that time returned to Japan, and were exciting a good deal of interest; and, hence they conclude, that it would have been impolitic to create fresh disturbances in the state by persecuting the Christians, and that that was the real cause of his feigning to be favourable to them. Whatever the motives of Taiko-Sama were, it is certain that he had expressed a desire to have the Franciscan Fathers in his dominions. For already Ferranda, the first ambassador to Manilla, before he left the city had delivered letters which plainly indicated that the emperor had given private, or secret, instructions to that effect, otherwise an ambassador would not have ventured to express himself so strongly. In these he says :—" I, Ferranda Gurimon, ambassador from the Japanese empire, certify that there are in our country a great number of Christians, who have received the first elements of the Christian faith, but who, for want of priests, are not yet sufficiently instructed. I know it will be highly agreeable to the emperor, my sovereign, if some ·of the Franciscan Order would go over to Japan. The emperor will admire their severe and strict way of living, and he will look upon their arrival in Japan as a great blessing. And, on account of their entire detachment from all earthly goods, they will be well received by the Japanese people. Therefore, I ask pressingly that some of those barefooted Fathers should be sent with me, promising them, in the name of my sovereign, that they shall be welcomed in Japan ; that no hurt shall be done to them, but that they shall be fully protected. And, moreover, I promise to bring them safely back again, should they desire to return."

These letters were very pressing,—the zeal of the good Fathers was burning in their hearts to fly to the assistance of those abandoned Japanese ; all the religious of the convent at Manilla offered themselves ; but yet, obedience to the higher authority, and humble submission to the Papal decrees, were uppermost before all other considerations. Pope Gregory XIII. had given to the Jesuit Fathers *alone* the care of the Japanese mission ; and so long as that decree was in vigour, Japan was shut against the zeal of the Apostolical Fathers. They calmly resigned themselves ; and prayed unceasingly that God would so dispose of this affair as to enable them to preach to the Japanese, both Christians and Pagans. The Jesuit Fathers had been greatly reduced in numbers, and were now very anxious themselves to obtain co-operators in their already too hard task of supplying the wants of so many thousands. But the good Jesuit Fathers could not act in opposition to the decree of Gregory XIII., nor annul its prohibitory force; and therefore the Franciscans resigned themselves to the will of heaven, and waited patiently to see whether God intended that the decree should be rescinded or not, by Papal authority. This soon afterwards was effected under the Pontificate of Pope Sixtus V. (a renowned member of the Franciscan Order), who, at least *partially*, revoked the decree promulgated by his predecessor of happy memory.

The second ambassador from Japan to the Philippine Islands brought more pressing letters from various Christians of the Japanese Islands. Those of Amanguchi wrote to the Franciscan Fathers at Manilla, "That they were 15,000, formerly baptised by Francis Xavier; but that they had now been twelve years without priests and without instruction. That they baptised each other at the house of a certain Christian called Joachim, in which were preserved a Cross, a Habit, and a Discipline, formerly belonging to Francis Xavier. That they had been driven from their native place on account of their faith. That only 400 had remained at their homes; and that they turned, with great confidence to the Philippine Islands to obtain Religious Brothers, of the Order of St. Francis, who would convert an immense number of the Japanese, because their manner of life was so much like that of the apostles of Christ. That Franois Xavier had often spoken in the highest terms of the Franciscans to the Christians of Japan. They also said that Tagunfa,

D

cousin of the Emperor, was a Christian, and that he was very desirous of getting the Franciscan Missionaries to instruct the people. That the Emperor had advised his cousin to return to the old idolatry of his ancestors, since no priests or guides could be obtained; but that the Prince had courageously replied, that he would rather die a thousand times, and be hewn into a thousand pieces, than abandon the Christian faith."

The Prince Justus Ucondino, a famous Christian general, who had been master of more than 80,000 vassals, had abandoned all his possessions, titles, and estates, and he persevered in the practice of the greatest poverty rather than return to Paganism. He could nowhere find a priest to instruct him and his people more fully in the Christian faith. He strongly insisted on having Fathers of the Franciscan Order to break the bread of life to the Japanese. Letters in quick succession arrived from Amacusa, all expressing the same desire. Brother Gonsalvus received a letter from Gracia, Queen of Tango, in which she thus expresses herself :—

" We pray ardently Brother Gonsalvus, as our dear son and brother, to come to instruct us. The need is very great. In eighty-nine cities and villages, which number each from 400 to 600 Christian families, there is but *one* solitary missionary; and because they cannot find any priest to administer to them, they are constantly enticed to return to the Pagan idolatry."

From other parts of Japan they wrote thus :—

" We Christians, who have been Bonzes (Pagan priests), turn ourselves to Brother Gonsalvus, of the Order of St. Francis, and we humbly beg of him to come and have compassion upon us, in the bowels of Jesus Christ. We abandoned our temples and revenues when we became Christians, and obtained the knowledge of the true God; and now we wander about in valleys and on mountains, without holding any intercourse with men. Knowing that the Religious of your Order are poor, and do not look for money, we ardently pray them to come over to these islands and gain souls for heaven, who now, through want of priests, are lost by thousands."

The Christians of Firando and Xiki made similar requests; for everywhere the want of priests was very great. In the meantime other letters were sent to the Pope, at Rome, and to Philip II., King of Spain, all repeating the same demand. From all these pressing letters it clearly appeared that God wished the Franciscan Order to exert its zeal in those countries. The Fathers became more and more solicitous for the work of the apostolate, and they all ardently desired to fly to the assistance of those forlorn creatures, who, like little children, asked for the bread of life, and there was no one found to break it to them; truly *"the harvest was great, but the labourers were few,"* and even these were checked in their zeal by the decree of Gregory XIII. The Fathers continued in prayer, and the Jesuit Missionaries pressed harder, with the proper authority, to obtain an opening for all Missionaries into Japan. God, at last, heard their united prayers; and Japan was, in a most extraordinary manner opened to the Franciscans.

The Governor of Manilla, beholding in what dangers the town was placed, and being unable to resist any invading force, and, moreover, being fully satisfied of the utter impossibility of resisting effectually the armies of Taiko-Sama, should he attempt to capture the island, he resolved under those circumstances to send a new embassy to the Emperor of Japan, to arrange a treaty of peace. He chose for this important and difficult work, Petrus Baptista, who had laboured for six years with great success amongst the natives of the Philippine Islands, and who was esteemed by every one as a very clever and a very holy man. The Archbishop in all matters of importance consulted him, and the Bishop of New Segovia had so great an opinion of Petrus Baptista, that he used to say " that he was worthy and sufficiently able to bear the tiara of Rome." He had

just been proposed as Bishop of Camerino, by King
Philip II. The Governor was so much the more
anxious to send Petrus, because the Emperor had
asked, through his ambassador, for the Franciscans.
Some of the clergy opposed themselves on the ground
that it was against the decree of Gregory XIII., but
the Archbishop having consulted his chapter, it was
unanimously resolved, that by the recent concession
of the reigning Pontiff, Sixtus V., the former decree
was limited, and that there was no real ground for
any valid opposition. However, Petrus Baptista,
whose affections were centred in heaven, and who
was thoroughly grounded in humility, perceiving the
opposition, declined the mission, alleging as an
excuse his utter incapacity for conducting any such
important political affair. But the Governor, being
now certified by the bishops that there was no fear
of opposition to the decree of Gregory XIII., and
hoping for good results, obliged Petrus Baptista to
undertake the mission to Japan. Father Petrus
Baptista, being thus obliged to undertake this mission
to Japan, began to turn over in his mind how he
should best make use of it for the salvation of so
many millions of the inhabitants of Japan. For, to
gain souls to heaven was his only aim and desire;
and it was only for that purpose he undertook the
embassy, as he well knew that if he could bring
about some treaty, that would insure happiness' to
the souls of the Japanese, the other matters would
soon settle themselves.

CHAPTER VII.

FATHER Petrus Baptista left the Philippine Islands on
the 21st of May, 1593. He went to Japan in quality
of an ambassador from the Governor, and of a commissary of his order; and he had for companions of his
journey, Father Bartholomew, Brother Francis de
Parilla, and Brother Gonsalvus. They all, after
having encountered many dangers, reached in safety
Ferando, in Japan. As soon as the Emperor, who
then resided with his whole court at Nangayu, was
informed of their arrival, he sent two of his court
officers to welcome them, and bring them over to his
palace. They remained some days in the palace,
where they were well treated; and they were visited
by all the influential personages of the court, until
the Emperor had fixed the day for their reception and
solemn audience.

The Emperor sent his servants with pavilion
chairs to carry them to court, as was the national
custom. But the Fathers, who, after the example of
their holy Father, St. Francis, rather wished to serve
others than be served by them, refused this honour,
and walked to the court. The Emperor received them
with great kindness and civility. He was surprised
at their poor Habit, and he was astonished at the great

simplicity which appeared in all their actions, and then, addressing his nobles and officers, he said :— " These men appear to be really sincere Christians ;" and he concluded by warmly thanking his ambassador " for having sent him these wonderful men."

Father Petrus Baptista then offered to the Emperor the precious gifts which he had brought with him from the Philippine Islands. The Prince received them with gratitude, and served them at table with his own hands. After he had conversed with them for some time, in a civil, meek, and princely tone, he suddenly changed his voice, and, assuming a proud, haughty, and commanding air, he made them understand, that " at his birth the sun had darted its resplendent beams upon his head, and that the gods, consulted by the soothsayers, had answered 'that he should become the master of the world;' that this prediction had already been fulfilled in regard to Japan, where he was the first who had solely ruled ; and, consequently, he demanded that the Philippine Islands should forthwith be ceded to him, and that their inhabitants should unhesitatingly submit themselves to his rule. And that in case his imperial demands were met by a refusal, he would, without delay, march at the head of an invading army of 200,000 disciplined soldiers, to conquer the islands and ruin their inhabitants, as he had already done with the Kingdom of Corea."—Father Petrus Baptista, seeing that now he had come to the point of his mission, and remembering that he had now to act as an ambassador for his king and master, Philip II. of Spain, recollected himself; and, without the least embarrassment, he replied, in a firm but amiable tone to the Emperor thus :—" His Majesty must bear in mind that he had asked, through his ambassador, not for the cession of the Philippine Islands, or the submission of their inhabitants, but

to make a treaty of peace and commerce. That on
those grounds he was unwilling to negotiate; but
if His Majesty persevered in exacting his demands,
he (Petrus) had no authority to give any reply to
such statements. That the King and the Governor
of the Philippine Islands could not be expected to be
prepared to meet such extraordinary demands, as it
was on different grounds that Taiko-Sama had
opened negotiations." The Princes and Ministers,
who surrounded the throne, were struck with these
frank and open declarations, given in such firm and
kind terms. The Emperor himself not being accustomed to hear such firm and manly speeches, was
completely baffled. Altering again his tone, the
Emperor replied—" That it was true, he had asked to
make a treaty of alliance with the people of the
Philippine Islands."

After this audience, the ambassadors were brought
into a large room, covered all over from bottom to top
with fine gold, and it was in this gorgeously fitted-up
apartment that they were to dine with the Emperor.
They cheerfully accepted the imperial invitation, in
the hope that it might give them a favourable
opportunity of treating further about those matters,
which were the objects of their double mission.
They were served at table by the Emperor's adopted
son. After dinner, Taiko-Sama remained with
them for a long time; and, whilst conversing in a
friendly and familiar manner with the Brothers,
he took the *Cord* of Father Petrus Baptista,
and giving himself a few strokes on the back, he
said: " Well, that discipline is rather biting." He
asked the ambassadors several questions on most
important subjects, which Petrus Baptista answered
so well, that the Emperor and the Princes were greatly
surprised and astonished to find so much wisdom and
science under the humble and coarse garb with

which he was clothed. They noticed in him, not only the simplicity and meekness of a Religious, but the astuteness and determination of the ambassador of a great king. By his shrewd intellect and cleverness he settled many difficulties which to them had appeared insurmountable; and the Emperor himself took, at every turn, more and more interest in them. He ordered the chief princes of his court to show them the town and all things worthy of special note; and he commanded them to lodge the ambassadors in their palaces, to provide for all their wants, and to take good care of them. He also commanded them to be honourably conducted to Miako, that they might inspect the capital and all its principal palaces.

Many of the princes of the court requested the Fathers to honour them by accepting invitations to dine at their tables; but they showed as much repugnance as was convenient in accepting those invitations, declining them, however, with as much politeness as possible. For they ever bore in mind that they still were Religious, bound by rule, and that their souls might suffer considerably if they permitted themselves to come, except in cases of great necessity, too closely in contact with feastings and luxury. Above all the other princes, Tonge, a great favourite of Taiko-Sama, showed them extraordinary affection, and he kept them during six months in his palace. The Emperor frequently inquired about the Fathers, and ordered the Prince to provide them well with wood and cloth. And, as the Fathers refused to wear more than one dress, the Emperor said that they *must* obey him, by wearing more cloth, if not they would most assuredly die from cold.

One day the Prince met them in the street, and taking off his overcoat would throw it over the shoulders of Petrus Baptista, but the Father declined the generous offer, and meekly induced the Prince to put it on again. The Emperor having given the government of Miako and two other princedoms to his cousin, he told him to frequently visit the Fathers, to converse with them, and to invite them to his table: but the Prince disobeyed the injunction of his sovereign and benefactor. The Pagans themselves greatly respected and honoured those good Religious, whom they saw despising all terrene goods, all pleasures, and all pastimes, and living in the strict observance of holy poverty, after the very manner of the Apostles of Christ. Wherever the Fathers went, they were received with great respect; so true is the beautiful language of Tertullian:—"*Anima naturaliter Christiana.*" The soul is naturally inclined to Catholicism, as appeared manifestly in the case of those Japanese Pagans, who could not help being moved by the example of those apostolical men.

Petrus Baptista and his companions were not idle; on the contrary, they took every opportunity of preaching to the idolators the true religion of Jesus Christ. Petrus laboured hard, and during the four years he remained in Japan, he performed mighty works by promoting the spread of Christianity, and, through it, true civilisation. His constant desire, his chief aim, was to gain souls to God. His great maxim was—"*Animas da mihi, cætera tolle tibi* — Give souls to me, and keep all other things yourself." Wherever he saw a few standing together, he ingeniously contrived to get near and throw out some sentiments which conveyed to their minds the knowledge of some of the great Christian truths. The Religious could not produce all the good they really wished for, neither could they take effective steps for gathering together large concourses of people, because they had no church or house in which they might instruct them and administer to them the Holy

Sacraments. On a certain day, the Emperor met them
in a street; he stopped and asked them how matters
stood with them, and whether they were in need of
anything. Petrus Baptista took this opportunity to
answer His Majesty, that they would be very glad if
His Majesty could let them have the house he had
promised them, because it was exceedingly difficult, if
not wholly impossible, to live according to their rule in
strange, secular houses. Taiko-Sama gave immediate
orders to the Governor of Miako, who accompanied
him, to give them a suitable place in which they
could, as Religious, live according to their rule; and at
the same time he granted them full permission to
found Convents of their Order in all places in his
realm. Petrus Baptista thanked His Majesty with
great warmth and humility, his eyes being suffused
with tears; and, with great love and much praise, his
heart poured forth grateful prayers to the great
God, who, by His wonderful providence, had so admi-
rably disposed all things for the good of Japan, and
who had so miraculously mollified the heart of the
barbarian monarch. On the evening of the same
day, the Governor went to Father Petrus, and gave
him a quiet and agreeable place in the town, sufficiently
large for the erection upon it of a church, and a convent and having a good garden, situated close to a river,
in the vicinity of which there resided a great number
of Christians. The buildings were commenced forthwith, at the joint expense of the Emperor and the alms
of the Christians; and even the Pagans themselves
contributed largely towards the swelling of the funds.
The pious Father, Petrus Baptista, pushed on the
work with great zeal, in order that the Church might.
be completed by the 2nd of August, 1594, and that
thus the faithful might gain the great Indulgence of
Portiuncula; and also because he ardently wished to
dedicate this Church to our Lady of the Angels, as

the first Church had been at Assisium. But as the work was being hurriedly carried on, with the intention of having it completed in a given time, on a certain morning, whilst the Saint was praying before the picture of our Lady, the following sentence, from the Book of Canticles, was suddenly imprinted at his feet: "*Daughters of Jerusalem, awake not, and do not awake the spouse before she wishes to be awoken.*" The holy man, greatly surprised, at once understood, by a special revelation from heaven, that God did not wish that the edifice should be pushed on to completion so rapidly, and finished at a period fixed by human prudence. He also was given to understand that the conversion of the heathen was properly the work of God, and not the work of man—a truth constantly verified in the Catholic Church. For the Catholic missionaries really convert nations, that is, change them from bad to good, from immoral to moral men. They really *regenerate* and civilise the nations, but then it is under the influence of the grace of God that they work these stupendous prodigies which even astonish our enemies! On the contrary, how barren are the results of *non*-Catholic missionaries; for if they can succeed in stuffing into the heads of the barbarians some notion of Christianity, it soon degenerates and becomes corrupt. The morals of the supposed converts do not improve by their coming in close contact with the teachers of pseudo Christianity; but, on the contrary, in very many instances their immorality becomes more refined and more intensified. No; real conversion is not properly the work of men, but the work of God, who merely employs men as a medium, or a channel, or an instrument, to convey to the souls of men the salutary grace of God, in the manner, way, or order established by His divine providence. Petrus Baptista, thus enlightened by God, who had so wonderfully manifested

His will, did not continue to push on with so great activity the completion of his church for the 2nd of August. It was, however, finished in a few weeks from that date, since we find that on the Feast of the Holy Founder, St. Francis, the 4th of October, the holy Sacrifice of the Mass was solemnly celebrated within its sacred walls for the first time. Father Petrus preached the opening sermon in a language, if not altogether correct, at least sufficiently clear to make himself understood by every one ; and his discourse told with great effect upon his hearers, all of whom witnessed the holy zeal which animated him, and felt their own hearts warmed by close contact with a man whose soul was burning with an ardent and unquenchable love for the salvation of souls. The Father, from that time, continued to preach every Sunday and holy-day. This was the commencement of the apostolical labours of the Franciscan Fathers in Japan ; their only aim was to save souls and sanctify them, and thus make them good and loyal citizens, and devoted subjects. Many Pagans came from all sides of the country to hear those new Apostles, and to behold their Convent, their Habit, and their humble and simple mode of life.

God was graciously pleased to show by miracles how pleasing their work was to Him, and how much He loved this church, dedicated to our Lady of the Angels. The following are the wonderful facts which the eye-witnesses both heard and saw, and communicated to posterity :—

When the Fathers hung their bell in the tower of the church, a strange thing happened which caused great astonishment, and even consternation, amongst the Japanese. Near the Church of the Friars there stood an idolatrous temple, having a bell of extraordinary proportions, which was renowned throughout the whole of Japan, and whose sound could be heard at the distance of many miles. But, as soon as the bell hung up in the tower of the Franciscan church was rung, the large bell of the Pagan temple would sound no more ; and though many plans were tried, and perseveringly repeated for some time, yet they never could succeed in restoring to this famous bell its use of speech. The Franciscan Fathers rang their bell for all the divine services with as much liberty and freedom as if they had been in a Christian country. The Emperor himself, moved by curiosity, came on a certain night to secretly watch the Religious in the choir, and to hear them sing the divine office; and he was exceedingly edified by the piety and devotion of the good Fathers. He admired the wonderful spirit of self-sacrifice which induced them to praise God and sing His office, at the very time that worldly people indulged in their pastimes and luxuries of all kinds. Oh! how different are the ways of God and the ways of the world!

Another wonderful event happened in the presence of the whole community, whilst they were assembled together in the choir. On the Feast of their holy Founder, St. Francis, October 4th, when there was not as yet any lamp in the church to burn before the Blessed Sacrament, there suddenly appeared four burning lamps, which signified the four years during which the Franciscan Fathers should preach the gospel quietly in Japan. Frequently were the songs of angels heard in this church, but especially on the Feast of All Saints, and of Christmas. God seemed to grant to it the same kind of favours which he had bestowed upon the little Church of our Lady of Angels at Assisium, for which our Holy Father and Founder felt such great devotion, and which became so renowned throughout the whole Christian world. Father Petrus Baptista spared no trouble in richly decorating the three altars in the church. On the high altar he placed a very precious tabernacle to conserve the Blessed Sacrament, which was constantly visited by the faithful, who bore towards it the warmest devotion. This devotion was wonderfully strengthened in the young Christians by the interposition of our Lord Himself.

A lady, tormented with doubts concerning the real presence of our Lord in the Blessed Sacrament, under the humble appearances of bread and wine, saw one day, whilst assisting at the holy Sacrifice of the Mass, a beautiful infant in the sacred species. This wonderful sight was the cause of the removal of all doubt; she ever after most firmly believed in the reality of the presence of Christ in the Holy Eucharist, and bore towards the Blessed Sacrament of the altar a most extraordinary devotion.

Another wonder, similar in kind, was witnessed by a Japanese, at the time the Fathers were making the procession in their Church. A lady, labouring under great affliction, and coming for consolation to the Church of the Fathers, saw our Lord, under the form of a little child, and bearing a heavy cross on His shoulders, inviting her to assist Him in bearing a cross whose weight so heavily oppressed Him. The lady, enlightened and comforted by this wonderful spectacle, understood that our Lord wished her to be patient, and to bear all her afflictions with great resignation.

Cosmas Toya, an old and fervent Christian gentleman, who was well acquainted with the Fathers, and most cordially devoted to them, managed all the temporal business of the Fathers, so as to leave them altogether occupied in their spiritual labours. This gentleman had a child covered all over with leprosy. He brought it to the Church, and Father Baptista completely cured it, by a peculiar grace from God. On the Feast of Pentecost, the miracle which happened at Jerusalem was renewed in this church. There appeared fiery tongues over all who were present in the Church. Many other wonders took place in the same Church, and a great many who were present during the manifestation of the above mentioned miracle, died martyrs; God having prepared them by degrees, and strengthened their faith by these extraordinary gifts. In every age, men have invariably borne witness that God has wrought great wonders for those nations who had never enjoyed the light of faith. For it seems to be a matter of necessity that God should show, by some extraordinary signs, the truth of His holy religion to those who have never had an opportunity of knowing that truth, and give them extraordinary graces in order that they might understand it, embrace it, and retain it. When, however, a people, or a nation, has once come in possession of the light of the Gospel, they can easily, by the ordinary means, ascertain where in reality the true religion is to be found; and, therefore, there will be no necessity for God to concur by the bestowal of extraordinary gifts. God never performs useless works to gratify the caprices of men.

CHAPTER VIII.

By the miracles which happened in the Church of
our Lady of the Angels, at Miako, and by the constant
preaching of the Franciscan Fathers, their good
example, their holy life—the Christians were again
animated with confidence, and their zeal became inflamed. Those who, under the first persecution, had
begun to shake and totter, became again firm; and
those who had fallen, raised themselves up again.
The holy man (Petrus Baptista) could not sufficiently
admire the disposition of divine providence, who
allowed him to build a church in the midst of the
capital of Japan, under the very eyes of the Emperor,
whilst, in other parts of the kingdom, the churches
were destroyed. It was really wonderful that whilst
the Jesuits—good, holy, and zealous missionaries as
they were—were strictly forbidden to show themselves,
the Franciscan Fathers continued to preach publicly
the Word of God, and to carry out their rule and
their holy practices without the least hindrance.

Were we to pause here, in order to investigate the
reasons why the Jesuit Fathers were not permitted to
appear in public, we should find no other motive
assigned than this, viz. :—the false and calumnious
assertion spread abroad by some influential Pagans,

and which in after times, until our own days, we
so frequently and so absurdly hear repeated even
by persons who, in many other respects, seemed
to be free from party bias, ill-feeling, or unjust
and unfair dealing; accusations with which the
Society of Jesus have been branded from the very
beginning—from its very origin—namely, " That they
only aimed at the attainment of an undue political
influence,—that by their supposed secret machina-
tions they laboured to upset every government in every
part of the world, for their own aggrandisement and
profit." There is nothing in the whole history of
that sacred and learned body of the Society of Jesus
to give the slightest ground for a belief in the truth
of such accusations. But, humanly speaking, it
happens unfortunately for those holy and learned
men that they bear the name of Jesus of Nazareth,
and acknowledge Him as their Chief. Now, as he
was accused by the Jews, and insulted, spit upon,
and crucified by them, it is only natural that His
true disciples should share in His Passion, and
become participators in His sorrows, even until the
Day of Judgment; when wickedness will be banished
from the earth, and when calumny and persecution
will be punished with everlasting torments, and
innocence and patient suffering be crowned with
perennial glory. Then will the hidden things of
darkness be brought to light, the secrets of hearts be
revealed, and disorder and confusion will give place
to concord and discipline. But so long as there is a
conflict between good and evil, the Jesuits and all
those who adhere lovingly and loyally to Jesus as
to their Chief and only Lord and Sovereign, will be
exposed to persecution. In Japan, the Jesuit Missionaries had converted a great many amongst the
highest classes, and this excited more particularly
the jealousy of the Bonzes, who were constantly

E

endeavouring to create prejudice in the Emperor's mind, and were secretly urging him to again unsheath the sword of persecution. On the other hand, the Franciscan Fathers, more simple and plain in their manner, and being obliged to practise strict poverty, were more closely united to the poor and to the great mass of the people, whose friends and protectors they have always been ; therefore, the Bonzes could not so well exercise their jealousy against them. In fact, the Franciscan Fathers were in possession of the largest amount of liberty; and Petrus Baptista with his brethren were constantly engaged in praising God, and in giving Him due thanks, for His wonderful goodness, and for the manifold benefits which He had so graciously and so profusely bestowed upon them. Petrus Baptista gently used the great influence he possessed, as ambassador, with the Emperor, and, at length, it came to pass that the Fathers of the Society of Jesus were permitted to labour openly and publicly for the spiritual good of the Japanese. By this concession religion made wonderful progress, and thousands of souls were rescued from the gulf of perdition, who were a little time before wavering and doubting, but who were quickly confirmed, as soon as the Fathers of the Society of Jesus and the Franciscans could use their mild influence upon their minds and hearts.

The Franciscans were accustomed to have, on the third Sunday of every month, in their Church, a Procession of the Confraternity of the Cord of. St. Francis, which Sodality Pope Sixtus V. (a Franciscan) had solemnly approved of, and enriched with very many Indulgences. The crowds of people who came to assist at this Procession, from all parts of the country, and from the many towns and villages which lay in the vicinity, were really immense ; the concourse was overwhelming. Those assembled enrolled their names as members, and religiously fulfilled the obligations with great devotion and perseverance, in order to gain the benefits of all the conceded Indulgences. Thus did the Fathers labour incessantly to convert the Pagans, and then to confirm them in faith by all the means at their disposal. From all parts did the people flock to their Church to assist devoutly at the Holy Sacrifice of the Mass, and to hear the sermons and instructions; and they brought with them statues of Christ, His Blessed Mother, and Saints, and Rosaries, which they had concealed during the persecution. In the beginning of the conversion of those Pagans, they had only been instructed in the rudiments, or first principles, of our holy faith, but sufficiently so to qualify them for the participation of holy baptism. Therefore, during the first year, they were not permitted to receive the Holy Communion; for that great Sacrament was not then administered until they were thoroughly instructed respecting those sacred mysteries, and might thus, with greater devotion, receive the body and blood of their Lord and Redeemer. As soon as they had become fully instructed, and had been made fully aware of the sublimity of the rite, and of the necessity for approaching to it with sincerity of mind and purity of soul; as soon as they fully appreciated its sublime dignity and transcendant holiness, they were with all joy permitted to feast upon the bread of Angels, and to become concorporeal with Christ.

The happy progress of the Christian faith in these Pagan islands appeared to some, even amongst the Catholics, a little too rapid and too public; and the holy Franciscan Fathers, whose only aim was to labour for God's glory, were admonished (now by one and then by another) to omit the public means of promoting religion, and everything else which might seem calculated to give offence to the Emperor. But the servants of God, who desired nothing but the salvation of souls, could not listen to these suggestions, which appeared to them to proceed from an excess of human prudence. They, therefore, persevered in their spiritual labours, and at the same time they enjoyed the friendship of the Emperor. They made wonderful progress; but the enemy of man's felicity being enraged, he was resolved to bring about their ruin. The Jesuit Missionaries had been the special objects of the hatred of the Bonzes; it now became the turn of the Franciscan Fathers. The Bonzes, or Pagan priests, who were very numerous in Japan, and whose number in Miako itself was 80,000, seeing that the influence of the Franciscan Fathers was become very great, and that they themselves had lost all consideration amongst their people, in proportion as these latter imbibed purer and holier principles of religion; and seeing, too, that the keen perceptions of the Japanese enabled them, by contrasting Paganism with Christianity, to easily discover the immorality, absurdity, and monstrosity of the doctrines and practices of the Bonzes,—moved by jealousy and anger, they plotted together to bring about the ruin of the Franciscan Fathers; and for that end they laid their accusations and complaints before the Emperor. But Taiko-Sama did not take any notice of their complaints, but, in reply to their charges, he said—that these Religious were good, and that he wished them to be left in quietness; that every one must be allowed to work out his salvation in the way he thought proper; and that these poor men did not seek any temporal advantage in the conversion of his subjects. As the Bonzes insisted, the Emperor asked them—"How many sects are there in my empire?" The Bonzes replied, "Thirty-five." "Well then," the Emperor replied, "if Japan can tolerate thirty-five different sects, it must also be able to tolerate thirty-six.

Leave these strangers in peace, and be as good as they are." The Bonzes finding that the Emperor would not listen to their accusations, turned themselves to the Governors of the city; and they persevered so long in making complaints, and in bringing forward false accusations against the Fathers to them, that the Governors at last refused to the poor Fathers an alms of corn, which the Emperor had ordered to be given to them. But God, who never forsakes or abandons his servants, procured for them, from the Christians, and even from some of the Pagans, the necessary daily subsistence, which was all they required. With this they were content; they desired no more. Being strict observers of their holy rule, they possessed nothing but their Habit, Church, and Garden, and their daily bread.

About this time, and in different periods, there arrived in Japan, Father Augustus Rodrigues, Marcellus Rabodineira, Jerome a Jesu, Franciscus Blanco, Martinus de Aguirre. Philippus de Las Casas and Joannes a Zamorra had previously brought presents to the Emperor from the Governor of the Philippine Islands. The saintly Petrus Baptista employed the whole night in giving thanks to God for the assistance He had sent him in this fruitful field, to labour for the salvation of so many souls. But Petrus Baptista also remembered that the Saviour of the world, when He sent His Apostles through the world to preach the gospel, also committed to their care and attention the sick and the miserable. The good Father, desirous of fulfilling that command of his blessed Master, began a work which was entirely new, and which was exceedingly pleasing to both God and man. Leprosy was a malady so common in Japan, that in the town of Miako alone there were not less than 3,000 infested with this awful plague. The Japanese were so cruel and barbarous towards those miserable creatures, that parents frequently killed their own children, and children their parents; men killed their wives, and wives their husbands, when they were infected with this disease. The most merciful carried their sick far away from home, into the fields and woods, and left them there without any assistance, that at least they might not see them die before their eyes. This cruel and barbarous treatment could not remain overlooked or unheeded by the compassionate Petrus Baptista. He at once began to build (with the alms he had received from Manilla, and also from the Christians of Miako and other places) two hospitals for the unfortunate lepers, who were carried on the shoulders of the Franciscans to their places, and they were taken care of by the Fathers themselves. He dedicated one of those hospitals to St. Ann, and the other to St. Joseph. He also established a school for the instruction of little children.

The two hospitals were immediately filled with 130 lepers, for all of whom Petrus Baptista and the other Fathers had procured beds and all other necessaries. The Fathers, kneeling down, with great charity and humility, washed and cleaned the filthy bodies of those neglected creatures; they dressed their wounds with respect and tenderness, remembering the wounds of our Saviour; they poured on them perfumed water to drive away the sickening and oppressive smell arising from their putrid sores; they exhorted each other by the holy thought that our Saviour had been bruised and wounded to cleanse away the leprosy of sin; they rivalled each other in zeal and attention to those under their care. They cured a great number of their patients, and Petrus Baptista, with the sign of the cross, frequently healed their wounds and restored them to perfect health. The zeal of the holy Religious soon stimulated others, secular persons, to join in this pious work. The first of the secular persons who devoted themselves to these great works of charity was Leo Carasuma, with his wife and all the members of his family; and blessed Paulus Suzughi. Leo took care of one hospital and blessed Paulus of another; and God rewarded their charity and zeal by bestowing upon both the crown of martyrdom. A great many of the recently converted Christians devoted themselves with admirable zeal to this holy work, so that, in those times, the fervour of the primitive Christians seemed to revive.

The copious alms which the Franciscan Fathers received for those hospitals was a continual miracle of divine Providence, who took a special care of the forlorn Christians in those barbarous lands, and gave to His servants all the requisites of life, with a super-abundance, for the support of the two charitable establishments. The Pagans themselves, moved by the sobriety of the Brethren, were moved to compassion, and they largely contributed towards their support. A young Japanese, who was sent every day by his mother to bring food to a Pagan priest, came to the hospital and gave it to the sick. God rewarded him for it, by bestowing upon him the gift of faith, and he soon became a Christian. Every one was surprised how those Fathers, strangers in Japan, could live and subsist, and, moreover, provide for the wants of the two hospitals. Of course those men were ignorant of the prediction of our Holy Father St. Francis, in which he said that "his children should always and everywhere find help and succour, provided they kept their rule." This has been fully verified during more than six centuries; and is being verified at this very time. A great number of the Pagans seeing the voluntary poverty, severity of life, contempt of the world and of all earthly goods, which appeared so conspicuously in the lives and manners of the Franciscan Fathers, acknowledged that there must be another life, and that it was solely to attain therein the summit of felicity, that the Fathers laboured with such zeal, and endured privations with so much patience. The example of all kinds of virtues exhibited in their conduct by the Fathers, their charitable works, their services in the hospitals without receiving any temporal emolument, opened the eyes of many heathens, and they resolved to abandon their idolatry and to become Catholics.

The Emperor seeing that those strangers took care of the most humble and the meanest of his subjects, and with such great charity, said to his courtiers :—" When I notice the praiseworthy works of those Christians, I must believe that Jesus Christ, in whom they believe and in whom they put their trust, is God; and also that there is another life, in which good works, austerities, penances, and all other charitable labours, are really rewarded ; solemn truths, to which we Japanese pay little or no attention." On another occasion he said :—" The doctrine of the Christians was very good, with the exception of the law of the sixth commandment : "—the one which forbids impurity and adultery. It was not surprising that this man, who like all other idolaters, placed his greatest happiness in the enjoyment of sensual pleasures, should reject this commandment, the observance of which appeared to him impossible. And in this he does not seem so far wrong, since he reckoned without the grace of God, to which, in his Pagan condition, he had no claim. Had he read the 2nd Epistle of St. Paul to the Corinthians, xii. 9, he would have seen that he could do all things in Him that strengthened him :—" *My grace is sufficient for thee.*"

When Petrus Baptista had now well arranged everything at Miako in the two hospitals and in his

own convent and church, he was anxious to extend
the same blessings to other cities also. He then left
Miako, in the company of Father Jerome, and went
to Nangazaki, a seaport town, in which there lived an
immense number of Pagans, and also several Spanish
and Portuguese Christian tradesmen and merchants.
The Christians earnestly entreated Petrus Baptista
to build a Convent. He, in virtue of the general
authority of the Emperor, which permitted the erection of religious houses in all parts of the Japanese
Empire, agreed with the Governor to take a goodly
spot of land outside of the town, which lay contiguous
to a small chapel which the Portuguese had founded
there in honour of St. Lazarus, and close to which
were also two hospitals. Father Petrus Baptista at
once ordered a few cells to be built, in which he could
live with his Brethren in a regular manner, according
to the rule of their Order. They began to preach in
the little chapel, and to perform in it all other services
and practices; and from early morning until late at
night, the little chapel was filled with devout Christians, and with Pagans who were desirous to witness
the new rites of Christianity. They were liberally
provided for by the inhabitants; not only were their
wants supplied, but they were in possession of sufficient means to support a large number of miserable
and sick persons in the two adjoining hospitals. But
all things were going on too prosperously; this state
of things could not always last. Such good works
must always expect to meet with opposition and
calumny. It was needful that they should be tried
by severe trials, difficulties, and contradictions. Three
months had now elapsed since their arrival in Nangazaki, and during that time they enjoyed much
calmness and peace. Their time was piously spent
in preaching to the Pagans, in converting them, and
in administering to the sick, with their usual care and

kindness. Now the storm began, for the devil excited men of evil passions to unfurl the standard of persecution, and to create a reaction in the public mind against them. The Governor, enticed by the Bonzes, expelled them from their quiet and harmless abode. Great was the sorrow of the Christians, and even of many of the Pagans, who loved them for their zeal and piety, and admired them for their goodness and simplicity; but heart-rending and indescribable were the lamentations of the sick, suffering in the hospitals, at being so suddenly deprived of their kindest friends. Father Petrus Baptista, before he left the convent, was for five hours in ecstatic prayer, and after that he recommended himself and all his Brethren, and also all the Christians and well-disposed Pagans, to the care of God's Providence; for they had only in view, in all their labours, the glory and honour of God and the salvation of their fellow men. God was pleased to reveal to His holy servant, whilst he was engaged in devout prayer, that an awful persecution would soon arise; and, in a rapture of mind, he said to Father Jerome : "Father, Father, let us fly from this place; let us go away from hence. Oh! what streams of blood will the pride and idolatry of Japan cause to be shed! But a glorious number, a splendid company, of the children of St. Francis shall remain in the soil of this city!" This prediction was subsequently fulfilled; for it was in that very town that he and his illustrious companions honoured God by a glorious martyrdom.

Before their departure from Miako, there arrived Joannes a Zamorra, whom the Father Provincial of the Philippine Islands had sent to visit them, and to ascertain what progress the Christian faith had made in Japan. He accompanied the Fathers to Nangazaki, and from that town he left for Spain. On his way to Miako, Father Petrus Baptista founded another

Convent in the town of Osaka, in which place the Governor provided generously the materials for the erection of the Convent, and he also supplied all the wants of the Missionaries. The holy man also preached in that town, and even in the Pagan temples, and with so much zeal and effectiveness, that two of the Governor's sons, with an immense number of people, embraced the Christian religion. He appointed Father Maguore the Superior, because he spoke the language of the country fluently, and by his apostolical zeal had much profited the souls of many.

Father Joannes a Zamorra, the visitor sent, as we have seen, by the Provincial from the Philippine Islands, having witnessed the conduct of the Fathers, their severe mode of living, their seeking for humiliations, their love of poverty, their utter contempt of the world, their constant labours during the day, their long prayers at night, and their severe disciplines—wrote thus to the Provincial :—

"I have witnessed those learned and holy men humble themselves at the feet of the lepers, kiss them, and clean and dress their wounds. I have seen in those servants of God the poverty, humility, and simplicity of our Holy Father, St. Francis of Assisium, shine in full lustre. I have noticed, with incredible satisfaction, our little Chapel at Miako raise its spire in the midst of two thousand Pagan temples. Wondering, I beheld the Fathers, though so very few in number, guide the Christians to heaven, and convert thousands of Pagans in the presence and under the influence of twenty thousand Bonzes, who are continually working and aiming at the destruction of Christianity."

Such was their life, such were their labours; full of fruit, and crowned with blessings. And thus before the persecution commenced, they put all their confidence in God, and they used the influence which they possessed with the Emperor, and which they gained in their quality of ambassadors, in order to promote God's glory and man's happiness. Their lives were holy, and they persevered in their holy work, following in every thing the inspirations of the Holy Ghost, whom they constantly invoked by prayer.

There have been historians who condemned the Fathers, if not for their apostolical labours, at least for the manner in which they had performed their sacerdotal functions. Those writers have endeavoured (though vainly) to prove that by their over-zeal the Fathers had provoked the persecution of the Emperor against the Christians. But we cannot find the least ground for this accusation. How can we condemn their zeal as too great, or tax it with indiscretion, unless we are prepared to condemn in like manner the zeal of the Apostles, who, after the coming down upon them of the Holy Ghost, on the day of Pentecost, rushed forth and preached Jesus Christ in the face of the Jews and the High Priests of the Synagogue? If the Apostles by adopting such modes did really err, we gladly and willingly follow in their wake, though at an humble distance, and are quite satisfied to partake of the obloquy which the world may heap upon them. St. Paul assures us that there will always be heresies, and consequently persecutions, that the good may be separated from the wicked. Truly did God infuse His Holy Spirit into those Evangelical and Apostolical men, and he animated them with heroic courage and dauntless intrepidity, to stand up and condemn with energy the Pagan idolatry, and to openly preach our Lord Jesus Christ and His doctrines, as the great St. Stephen, the Proto-martyr, did in the presence of the High Priests and the Jewish rabble. The case simply stands thus—those holy Religious, having before them the examples of the apostles and of St. Stephen, endeavoured to imitate them, and to walk as closely as possible in their footsteps. No Christian could have temerity enough to condemn the Apostles and the holy deacon: therefore, no Christian can lawfully condemn the Franciscan Fathers, whose only aim was to promote the pure worship of God and to save men's souls. God has appointed only one way to heaven, and it is most reasonable to conclude that if men, duly authorised, adopt such means as the Apostles of Christ adopted for leading men with certainty into that way, and for securely keeping them therein, they have no right to be condemned; for God who is essentially holy would not sanction such means by miraculous interpositions, if they were displeasing in His sight. God is always the same, and He is uniform in all His works. For peculiar circumstances He sends peculiar men; He animates them with His Spirit; and, being thus moved and inspired, they rush forward with promptitude and alacrity, fearless of consequences; for no human prudence is of any value in the estimation of God.

The Franciscan Missionaries were now distributed in those two Convents of Miako and Osaka, and they prepared themselves by incessant prayer and bloody disciplines, for the coming struggle and martyrdom, which they knew by revelation were hanging over the Christians of Japan.

CHAPTER IX.

FLAVIUS JOSEPHUS tells us what wonderful signs occurred before the ruin of Jerusalem. The same kind of portents have been witnessed, in succeeding ages, before the advent of great events. It would be unwise to reject these signs as impossible things, as mere chimeras, or as being improbable, on the ground that they are striking events, singular phenomena, or wonderful occurrences. God can work them, and when they have been witnessed by credible vouchers, by men of character, and are handed down to us through the usual channels, we must, as rational beings, take them as historical facts, without criticising more particularly, and accept them as we do every other historical fact. Those wonderful occurrences are warnings sent by God, and intended by Him to bring men to reflection, in order that they may be rescued from their evil ways, or to prepare and strengthen others for the coming struggle. .

In the year 1586, the most awful events took place in Japan, which were evidently the harbingers of the first persecution. In the cities of Miako and Saccai there was so great an earthquake (which was felt during the space of forty days), that a great number of houses and a magnificent Pagan temple fell into ruins. Another city, in the Kingdom of Vomi, was half swallowed by the earth, and the other half was burned down. Another city was buried under the waters of the sea, and all its inhabitants perished. A strongly-built and well-fortified castle, situated on the top of a hill, sank altogether into the ground, and was replaced by a deep pool of water. In other places the earth was cleft open, and exhaled such deadly smells that nobody could approach and endure their nauseous and suffocating odour. Soon after the appearances of these signs the first persecution took place against the Jesuits.

In the year 1589, other signs occurred, which we may consider as the forerunners of the second persecution. On the 28th of December there was found in the village of Obama, which was distant three miles from Arima, in the midst of a tree, a beautiful cross of a brownish colour. About six months before this occurrence took place, the King of Arima, recently converted to the Catholic religion, had had a vision, in which he was told that soon the Sign of the Saviour should be found in a miraculous manner, within the limits of the kingdom. As soon, therefore, as this wonderful emblem was discovered, the King, the Queen, and the royal children, came thither to witness the presence of the miraculous Cross. The King remembered his vision, but to make himself sure that there was no deception, he got some clever Pagan naturalists to report whether it could be naturally explained that a Cross should be found in the midst of a tree ; or whether there were not signs that it had been fixed there by a natural contrivance to deceive. When those men had reported that they did not know of any natural force by means of which the Cross could be placed where it was found, and that it could not have been, and consequently had not been placed there by human hands or by natural appliances; the King, again mindful of his vision, became fully

convinced that *this* was the Sign of their Holy
Saviour, which in that vision he was told should soon
make its appearance. He carried it over to Arima
with great respect, and put it in a very precious
shrine. The Christians came from far distant places
to pay their respects to this Sign of their Saviour.
This Cross, with the evidence it conveyed, was so
wonderful that in the year 1590, 11,500 Pagans were
baptized and became Christians ; they persevered,
and were remarkable for their zeal and piety. It is
reported, but without sufficient evidence or authority,
that several other crosses, much like the crosses
upon which the Japanese Martyrs were crucified,
were found in various parts of the empire. Such
reports were particularly current in the neighbour-
hood of Facunda ; but as we have not unques-
tionable evidence upon the subject, we will not
enlarge upon it. We leave it entirely to the judgment of our readers ; and they will either believe or
discredit those reports, in consequence of the presence
or absence of those grounds of probability which are
sure to obtain the assent of the mind.

More awful and terrible were the signs which
happened in 1596, the year before the breaking out
of the persecution. There fell at Miako such a
quantity of red earth, which appeared as if saturated
with blood, that the roofs of the houses, the streets,
and the fields were covered with it. In the month
of August, of the same year, there was a shock of
an earthquake, which, however, did not cause great
damage ; but in September it was repeated with such
violence, that men had no time to escape, and were
buried by thousands, under the ruins of their houses.
On the same night the temple of Daybut, which was
the most precious and sacred in the whole empire of
Japan, fell in, and the idols Daybut and Focoto were
smashed to atoms. When the Emperor heard this

news, he said that Daybut was not a good god, since
he could not protect himself in his own house.
Another temple of the palaces of Dayri also fell in,
and all the idols were broken into pieces; and of the
eighty Bonzes attached to this temple, only two
escaped; all the others were buried beneath its
ruins. In the same manner the temples of Osaka
and Miako, with their surrounding palaces and dwell-
ing-houses, were thrown down. Moreover, at Miako
there fell in twenty very large houses, reputed the
most splendid buildings in the town, which were
inhabited by Bonzes, who, with an immense number
of other Pagan idolaters, perished in the ruins. The
greatest treasure lost on this awful occasion was a
gorgeous palace, which was generally valued at three
hundred millions of golden marks.

The population being now in great consternation
and fear, there was felt, on the 5th of September,
another great shock of an earthquake. The roaring
of the wind was so terrible that hell seemed to have
opened its gates, and to have sent out legions of
devils for the purpose of turning the world upside
down. Every one fled from the houses into the fields,
whilst a most piercing and heart-rending cry arose
from all quarters and filled the air. Parents lamented
the loss of their children, and children were crying
for their parents, and friends wept over friends swallowed up by the gaping earth, or buried under the
ruins of the fallen houses.

The city which suffered most severely was Fuscino,
where the Emperor had displayed his luxury in the
most princely and gorgeous manner. Four magnificent
palaces fell in with an awful noise; and not a single
idolatrous temple or dwelling-house of the Bonzes
remained standing. One hundred and seventy of the
Emperor's wives, or concubines, were buried under
the ruins of the Harem, and more than 20,000 of the

F

inhabitants lost their lives. The Emperor fled away in his night dress, and dwelt for some time on the mountains; all the nobles left the city, and sheltered themselves in the fields.

It was a wonderful thing to see, that during the continuance of those awful calamities all the Convents and houses of the Franciscan Fathers and Jesuits, and the dwellings of all the Christians remained unhurt, and a great many of the Pagans went to them to obtain shelter under their roofs. Other calamities occurred by the overflowing of the sea, which destroyed whole cities and villages; and more than 30,000 individuals perished in the small town of Saccai. Hailstones in the form of darts fell in immense quantities, and completely destroyed all vegetables. A fearful comet, red as blood, appeared in the air, and brought on such intense darkness that the people could hardly see the ground.

In the Church of the Franciscan Fathers at Miako, there was a magnificent statue of our Holy Father St. Francis, which sweated an immense quantity of blood; and this prodigy was looked upon by the Fathers as a sure sign that they should soon shed their blood in defence of the faith. All those signs happened before the eyes of the Fathers, who everywhere lent the greatest assistance to the forlorn people. They spent day and night in comforting the desolate widows and the orphan children; baptised many Pagans, and brought an immense crowd of sinners to repentance. All the people, seeing death before their eyes, were thunderstruck on beholding the calmness and resignation which appeared so conspicuously in the conduct of the Franciscan Fathers, amidst the horrors of the general devastation, and they resolved to join themselves to the religion which the Fathers preached and practised. The holy men thought that they could not be sufficiently thankful to God for such a manifestation of His power, by which He showed His hatred of idolatry, and His burning love for the souls of men. To make compensation for the destruction of so many bodies in the awful catastrophes which seemed to threaten the utter ruin of all Japan, innumerable souls were gained to God, who in more prosperous times would have sunk into eternal perdition.

All those calamities, however, did not make any impression upon the Emperor, or upon the surviving Bonzes, who were now busier than ever with the Emperor, trying to induce him to root out and banish that wicked race, the Christians. Seeing their own temples in ruin, and the Churches of the Christians standing whole amidst the general wreck, and daily filled with faithful and sincere worshippers, the Bonzes began to rage like frenzied men ; they slowly, and by degrees, rebuilt their dwellings and their temples ; and, as usual, they charged the Christians as the wicked authors of all the calamities of the times ; and they proclaimed everywhere that the injured gods of the nation had united to punish the Japanese for having forsaken the ancient worship, and for having permitted the abominable Christians, the authors of all the calamities that afflicted the world, to have a footing amongst them. They worked hard and unremittingly with the Emperor, in order to gain their point, taking hold of every opportunity to embitter his mind and to make him execute the decree, which he had sanctioned and issued a few years before, for the general extirpation of the Christians from the whole of the empire of Japan. The Emperor, however, still continued to waver and to be undecided

It is also recorded that the Dutch merchants, still aiming at their favourite scheme of obtaining a monopoly of all the commerce of the country, were

constantly labouring to excite the worst passions of
the Japanese against the Spaniards and Portuguese;
and that they were not scrupuluous in disseminating
all sorts of calumnies against the Christians in general.
The Bonzes, on the other hand, making use of every
report, of every circumstance, and of every word which
they heard, redoubled their accusations against the
Christians in the presence of the Emperor. Very
opportunely for their wicked purpose, they found a
powerful instrument in the impious, immoral, and
cruel Jacuinus, who did not care for God or law, and
whose only happiness consisted in the gratification
of his carnal passions. He, however, pretended to be
religious and to worship the idols; and, as a seeming
proof of his piety, he rebuilt at his own cost some of
the fallen temples. This Jacuinus is the very same
individual that ten years before had excited the first
persecution against the Jesuit Fathers. Whilst he
was busily engaged in re-edifying the Pagan temples
for the worship of the devil, he could not, without
becoming furious, behold the wonderful progress
which the Catholic Religion had made. He feared,
and not without good reasons, that the light of the
Gospel would soon dispel the darkness of Paganism,
which then covered Japan. The Bonzes also urged
him constantly and energetically to use his influence
with the Emperor. Jacuinus strove to make the
Emperor believe that the Christians were not good
subjects, that they were not loyal, that they hated
the Emperor, and were constantly plotting for the
overthrowing of his throne. It was a long time
before the Emperor would listen to this false and
impious accusation. He had seen, and daily saw,
how faithful the Christians were to his throne, and
how by means of apostolical preaching morality had
improved in his dominions; and he was compelled to admire the patient zeal of the holy Mis-

sionaries in their labours for the relief of the poor and miserable of his empire. However, Jacuinus and the Bonzes did not lose courage; and here again we have the truth of the old proverb realised, that " *a constantly repeated lie finishes with passing current as a truism."* How often have we not experienced it? and do we not even now experience it, in the every day occurrences of life? It is also to be noticed, that from the very beginning of Christianity down to our own times, all the enemies of the Catholic faith have always accused its professors of disloyalty; and whatever they have done to prove the contrary, it has always remained a standing objection. We have invariably pointed to the Gospel maxim: "*Render to Cæsar the things which are Cæsar's; and to God the things which are God's."* This rule has always been, and is still, faithfully observed by all practical Catholics; for, in fact, it is of indispensable obligation, and the greatest care has been taken in every age to enforce its observance.

Jacuinus, in order to instil with more certainty his false accusations into the mind of the Emperor, and to make them pass off as real truths, found an excellent occasion in an inconsiderate and untruthful speech of a pilot of a large ship, which unfortunately had been shipwrecked on the coast of Japan. The ship was heavily laden with silver and other merchandise : she was large and was called " Philippus." She had sailed from the Philippine Islands for New Spain, on the 22nd of June, 1596. In this ship there were several Religious, of whom four were Augustinians, one a Dominican, and two Franciscans: the two last, were Brothers Philippus de Las Casas and Joannes a Zamorra. When they were on the open sea, Brother Joannes foretold that in a few days a most terrible hurricane would arise; and on the fourth day the prediction had its accomplishment. They were obliged to throw overboard a great quantity of goods, and they lost the masts with the sails. The gale was a most terrific one, and the whole of the sky was covered with black clouds. In the direction of Japan there appeared all of a sudden a large cross; it was very brilliant and white at first, but it was soon changed into a blood-like colour, and became enveloped in a thick black cloud. The fear caused by the tempest overwhelmed the crew and passengers, and, as if struck by lightning, they remained almost lifeless by the appearance of such a portentous sign; they were, for a time, deprived of the use of speech, and looked as spectre-like as the pale corpses of the dead. The ship being deprived of masts, sails, and helm, floated on the foaming ocean during three long months; but being under the special guidance of divine Providence, she at last reached the harbour of Urundo, in the Province of Cosa, in Japan. The Doimo, or Prince, of that country was soon made acquainted with the fact, and he immediately dispatched two hundred boats, which brought the galleon* into the haven. The Spaniards prepared a very grand and rich present of silk, cloth, pearls, and jewels, and ordered Brother Joannes to offer it to the Emperor; but Taiko-Sama, warned by Jacuinus that the ship was laden with rich treasures, refused the offer, and commanded that the crew should be taken prisoners, and that all the cargo should be seized for his use. He despatched for this purpose a certain man named Maxita. The pilot was full of sorrow at the idea of losing his ship and the treasures it contained; and when, therefore, Maxita was on the point of executing his orders, he (the pilot) thought of using an expedient by which he might be able to prevent the intended

---

* A large ship, with four or five decks, now only used by the Spaniards.

seizure. The wickedness of this man was the source
of the most unfortunate consequences, and the evil
effects of his cruel treachery are severely felt at the
present time. His calumnies have been frequently
used since his time to blacken the characters of the
holy Missionaries; and they form a portion of the
staple charges that are periodically brought forward
to malign those apostolic men, who, sacrificing ease,
wealth, family ties, and all that the world admires
and loves, go forth duly commissioned to preach the
Gospel of Christ to bad Christians, to Jews, to
heretics, and to Pagans. The misguided and un-
principled pilot, in the presence of the Minister of
the Emperor, in order to frighten the Japanese, dwelt
forcibly upon the great power of the King of Spain,
who had immense possessions in Europe, Asia, and
Africa, and he drew particular attention to the extent
of Philip's possessions in America. He pointed out
minutely and with great distinctness, on a large map of
the world, each separate possession of his royal master.
All the Japanese were amazed at the recital of this
wonderful narrative; but the shrewd Maxita could not
help asking him how His Majesty the King of Spain
had contrived to obtain so many possessions. The pilot
saw that his words had made a very deep impression
on the minds of those present; but he became much
confused when Maxita put his plain and natural
question. Labouring under great mental excitement,
he found it difficult to make a ready and appropriate
reply. He was a man of the world, forgetful of God's
presence and his own accountability. He loved his
ship and the treasures which formed her cargo, with
an inordinate attachment. To strive by lawful means
to save his property and whatever else was given him
in charge, from the cupidity of a tyrant, so far from
being a criminal act, was a Christian duty. Had he
spoken truthfully he would have acted rightly, and as

a consequence, he might, or might not, have lost his
all. The pilot was obliged at length to speak; and
what did he say? Unfortunately for his soul's welfare,
and indescribably more so on account of the millions
of souls who, through his nefarious conduct, have
since been eternally lost, he forgot every regard for
truth, and wholly rapt up in his riches and absorbed
in the one idea of how he could save them, he basely
and calumniously replied, that " Nothing is more easy
of attainment than for our Kings to take possession
of others' lands *ad libitum.* They first send thither
Missionaries, who prepare the people for intended
changes. And when those have sufficient numbers
around them, well initiated in the plot, then our
Kings send armed men, who join themselves to the
converted heathens, and supply them with arms and
the other munitions of war, and thus do the Kings
easily attain their ends." Against this false state-
ment the whole of the crew, with the passengers,
indignantly protested. They declared that their
Kings had no such policy, that missionary zeal was
wholly directed to the spiritual good of men, and the
salvation of their immortal souls. But the pilot's
words had made an impression: the die was cast, and
the malice of an immoral man, whose heart was
centred in self, was the certain cause of one of the
most sanguinary persecutions on record; exceeding
in intensity and duration of time, if not in extent,
those which raged under Nero and Diocletian. Men
of reflection and of unbiased minds, irrespective of
country or of creed, will readily admit that the pilot's
tale carried on its front the impress of absurdity and
impossibility. What would the Methodists say, if
such imputations were thrown against their missionaries in foreign parts? Would they not shrink back
with horror, and protest in the face of heaven and
earth that such charges could only have received their

inspirations from the Prince of Darkness? Or, if we supposed that the British Bible Society only aimed at material advantage, and used the Bible as a means to revolutionise other countries, in order that England might find a pretext to annex to herself other portions of the world, would not the religious world in England rise up *en masse*, and solemnly denounce the calumny? There might seem to be a reason why England, which is a powerful nation, and whose Government might not scruple to use religion as a means—a stepping-stone—for the acquisition of other men's territories, should by brute force upheld by State chicanery, act so, and especially since her Government is at the head of Protestantism as well as of political affairs. But laying aside conjectures, and avoiding any reflections that would lead to angry controversy or endless recriminations, and confining our views to the household of faith, we positively assert that no Catholic Emperor, King, or Queen ever aided the transmission of Apostolical Missionaries to heathen countries without leaving them free to carry on the work of God, which is the salvation of souls. Our evangelical heroes are not sent by Kings or Potentates of any degree, for these are as powerless to give spiritual faculties or jurisdiction as the dead who have slept for ages. They are sons in the church, not fathers. To Peter was given the keys, not to Herod or Tiberius. Those keys remain, and will always remain until the consummation of ages. In an unbroken line, during eighteen centuries, Peter's voice has been heard in his successors. Peter transmitted the keys with all his powers to his successor. They have passed successively from one to another, and in our times Pius IX. firmly holds them. The succession will continue to the end; and the keys will be transmitted down to him who shall occupy the place of Peter at the sounding of the last trumpet.

Then the tri-partite church, the Militant on earth, the Suffering in Purgatory, and the Triumphant in heaven, shall be united in one ; and as Christ will be for evermore the *visible* head of His *united* church, the succession of Peter will end, and the keys will be given back to Him who originally gave them.

Our Missionaries, then, go with God's blessing, and under obedience to the Pope their spiritual Father, because he stands to us on earth in the place of Jesus Christ, and because he is the source of all spiritual power and jurisdiction ; for he it is who alone has received the plenitude of authority in the Church of God. All true Missionaries, then, are sent immediately or mediately by him, and thus commissioned they go to some designated locality to labour and to suffer, and they never acquire any temporal advantage; but, on the contrary, they cheerfully sacrifice every thing, even life itself, for the propagation of the religion of God, and for it only. If they return at all, they do return enriched with the spoils of poor nations, the souls of whose inhabitants they have snatched from the jaws of hell. They water, in many instances, with their sweat and blood the soil of the lands blessed by their apostolical labours. Their object is to sow the seed of Gospel Christianity ; and, unencumbered by earthly riches, they place all their confidence in Divine Providence.

However rash, inconsiderate, and untruthful was the pilot's speech, the false accusation, which was immediately contradicted by the Missionaries themselves, as well as by the ship's crew, became, nevertheless, the spark which ignited the elements of destruction, and gave rise to that furious persecution which deprived Japan for centuries of the true faith; plunged back its people into all the abominations of Paganism, with its idolatry and superstition, and caused the eternal ruin of millions of souls. Well, then, may we observe that no intellectual effort of the most enlightened minds can calculate the immense amount of mischief which an evil tongue, or even an unguarded speech, may produce. It is a secret which will remain unrevealed until we appear before the judgment-seat of God. How true is the language of inspiration : *"He who has not offended with the tongue is a perfect man."*

Maxita, having returned to Jeddo, related to the Emperor, Taiko-Sama, in the presence of Jacuinus (who, we can easily imagine, rejoiced to find this pretext for redoubling his entreaties with the Emperor to extirpate the Christian race), the whole of the lying tale narrated by the pilot. A sardonic smile appeared on his countenance, and he made the Emperor feel that his warnings had been wisely given. Jacuinus had laboured long, he was now successful ; for the proud and ambitious Taiko-Sama at length broke out into a frenzy of rage, and said : " Well now, how has it come to pass that my states should be filled with traitors who conspire against me, and secretly league with others to deprive me of my kingdom ? And their number daily increases. I ordered them in the beginning to be expelled, or put to death, but through pity, and on account of their age, I tolerated them. I shut my eyes on many others, because I believed them to be quiet and good citizens, incapable of fostering any evil design; and those men are the serpents which I have nourished in' my own bosom, and, in requital for my protection and generosity, they have been inciting my subjects to become my enemies. But they will soon learn, to their cost, what it is to have dealings with Taiko-Sama." After he had spoken thus, he swore the most frightful oaths, by which he bound himself to destroy every one of them, and to expel the Portuguese merchants and all their dependents. The ·fire was now enkindled, and we shall next be called upon to witness a most terrible tragedy.

The rumour of this sudden event was soon spread, and great alarm was created amongst the Christians, who were now fully aware of the lot that awaited them. The dark and heavily-charged cloud that hung over their heads had suddenly burst, and like electricity had spread the fire from one end of Japan to the other. But God, who is always present to comfort and to strengthen His servants, had so arranged matters, by His ineffable goodness, that just at that very critical time the Bishop of Japan had arrived at Miako, to reassure the fearful, and, by administering the holy Sacrament of Confirmation, to fortify the Christians for the coming struggle. The holy Prelate had little or no repose either by day or by night. The faithful flocked from the most remote parts of Japan to receive the holy Sacrament, in order that their souls might be prepared to face the persecution. But even this great concourse of the Christian people at Miako was wrongly interpreted by Jacuinus, and was by him reported to the Emperor, who, wholly blinded by passion, lost all his good qualities, and, as if all the infernal spirits had possession of him, he, uttering the most horrid curses and blasphemies, urged on the extirpation of the Christians. Forgetful of the former liberty he had granted to the Missionaries, he gave immediate orders for their arrest and execution. His orders were promptly obeyed.

CHAPTER X.

TAIKO-SAMA thus moved by infernal rage, called one
of his Ministers, Ufioio, and reproached him most
severely for having given protection to the Christians.
He upbraided him for having shown them much cour-
tesy, and he was very angry because the Minister's
father, Faxega (who was sincerely and devotedly attached to the Fathers) had not only given them his
countenance, but had also been their benefactor.
The Minister replied : " That his father had treated
those Missionaries as ambassadors of their own empire, and that in that quality they appeared to his
father to be worthy of honour and respect ; but, that
as far as he himself was concerned, he had watched
their movements, and had noticed with astonishment
that they preached their doctrine and made a great
number of proselytes. That he had observed all their
public acts, and had made a list of all those who
seemed to be acquainted with the Missionaries, and
to be in close relation with them. He had even given
the Missionaries good advice, requesting that they
would desist from their practices, but they did not
make any account of anything he said to them. They
have also neglected the remonstrances of Genifuin,
the Prime Minister of your Majesty." The Emperor
at once ordered the list to be produced ; he read it,

and immediately gave his orders, by which he commanded Gibonoshio, another of his Ministers, to put guards at the doors of their houses for the purpose of securing them.

This order of the Emperor was executed on the evening of the 8th of December, the Feast of the Immaculate Conception of the Blessed Virgin Mary; and under that title the special Patron of the Franciscan Order, and to which mystery also, the Martyrs had a great devotion, as true children of the Holy Patriarch St. Francis. On the morning of the 9th of December, the Franciscans found themselves prisoners in the Convent, in which had been wrought so many wonders. All their names were taken down, and the Fathers were closely watched as if they had any wish to escape, who desired so much, and longed so ardently for, the crown of martyrdom. The Emperor issued a mandamus ordering *all* the Christians to be put to death; but their number was so immensely great that in the town of Miako alone four thousand voluntarily offered themselves to suffer and to die for the defence of the Christian faith. The Pagan Princes and Ministers had compassion on this great number, and especially because two sons of the Minister Genifuin were Christians; and, therefore, they besought the Emperor that he would be satisfied with the shedding of the blood of the Franciscan Fathers, and their principal and most zealous friends. On the other hand, Ufioio with Gibonoshio insisted that the Convent of the Jesuit Fathers should be surrounded by guards, because they had proved themselves to be as zealous propagators of the forbidden faith, as the Franciscans themselves. A quarrel, therefore, arose between the two ministers; but Gibonoshio feared to displease the Emperor, because a certain Jesuit Father, named Rodriguez, acted as Rebima to the Emperor, and was rather a kind of favourite. The Minister was, therefore, afraid to irritate the Emperor by placing guards around the Jesuit Convent. Fearing, however, on the other hand, to displease Ufioio, the great favourite of the Emperor, they sent a guard for the sake of appearance, but not with the intent of using present action. In the Franciscan Convent there were, at the time the guards were placed there to secure the arrest of the inmates, two children—one aged twelve years, was named Lewis, and the other, named Anthony, was thirteen. They could have escaped, liberty was even offered to them, but no; those courageous boys, who had during several months served the most of the Fathers, would not leave them, but preferred martyrdom, and behaved most bravely and heroically, as we shall see in the sequel.

The Emperor also gave strict orders to set guards upon the Convent at Osaka, which command was executed without delay, and Father Martinus de Aguirre with three others were taken prisoners. The saintly Father Petrus Baptista, as soon as he heard that the Fathers at Osaka were taken prisoners wrote to Father Martinus de Aguirre as follows:—" It is with consolation I hear how God strengthens you to suffer for Him, and also to comfort the Christians around you. God gives us the same grace; we also are prisoners, and our Convent is guarded both within and around. We all deem it a great favour to be chosen to suffer for God. I was warned that the sentence of death was passed against us, and that we were to be executed the next morning; therefore we spent the whole night in prayer and in hearing confessions, to prepare ourselves in a worthy manner for this great favour. I offered up the Holy Sacrifice of the Mass an hour before daylight, and distributed the Holy Communion to all our brothers, and to fifty Christians, who all, with tears of joy in their eyes, thanked God

for the great grace now so singularly bestowed upon
them, by preparing for them the glorious crown of
martyrdom. Brother Gonsalvus preached a most
beautiful and moving sermon, to give them courage
to suffer cheerfully. All present, in raptures of joy,
unanimously exclaimed 'that they wished to have a
hundred lives, to lay them all down for Jesus Christ,
who suffered so much for us.'"

"After Mass a great many Pagans, and amongst
them some ministers of justice, entered the convent,
and searched everything minutely and scrupulously.
Soon after the Governor came with other servants. We
were then told that they had cords and chains to bind
us. Who can express the joy we all felt, and the
thanks we rendered to God, that now the fortunate
hour was come—that we were to shed our blood for
Him, and so enter into His glory, through this short
struggle? But great was our disappointment, for
they only took our Interpreters, Leo, Paul, Bona-
venture, Gabriel, and Thomas, whom they strongly
bound and led to the prison. Our separation was a
cruel one, and we all ardently desired to join them.
Those heroic men went cheerfully through the streets,
preaching the Christian doctrine to the surrounding
multitude. Their cheerfulness surprised the Pagans.
They have already written to us from their prison
that it is certain they must die, and that they wish
to have a slow death, so as to suffer much and a
long time for our dear Lord Jesus Christ. We were
all very sorry that we were not as yet found worthy
to suffer when we saw the Judge and the Ministers of
Justice depart from us. But we still live in good
hopes, and we endeavour by prayer and penance to
make ourselves worthy of the grace of martyrdom.
The soldiers still watch us very closely, and all
Christians are forbidden to approach us. Pray for
us, my dear Father, as we do for you. Let us put

all our confidence in God's goodness, not forgetting that it is *only now* we begin to follow (at an humble distance) after the pattern of the Apostles. God also gives us wonderful comfort, strength, and zeal, to suffer all kinds of torments for His glory. We thus rejoice to have been found worthy to suffer at last something for God."

Whilst the good Father was writing those lines, the Emperor held a council meeting; there also appeared Gibonoshio and Gemonogis, and also Faxega and his son Ufioio. Taiko-Sama severely rebuked the Governors of the city, for having neglected his orders and allowed those strangers to preach the doctrine of Jesus Christ, and baptize a great number of the Japanese. Gibonoshio answered, " That only the Franciscans had transgressed his orders; that the Jesuits had been reserved in their zeal, and had not made any proselytes, except, perhaps, the old Father Organtine." Faxega felt great compassion for the Missionaries, though he was a Pagan, but being unable to excuse, in the eye of the law, the Franciscans, he endeavoured, at least, to excuse the Jesuits; and he even hoped that the Emperor would yet change his mind, and grant grace to the Franciscans, or at all events be content with their banishment. The Emperor suspended his last decision, and sent his Ministers home; but as his countenance indicated that his passions were raging within him, and that nothing but blood would satisfy, the Ministers were convinced that the sentence of death would be passed upon the prisoners : they, however, were not wholly without hope. The next morning the Emperor had come to a decision. He sent for Gibouoshio, who entered the Emperor's apartments just as the monarch was considering about the erection in a gorgeous style of a new palace; and without much apparent disturbance, he felt

G

satisfaction in uttering these short words :—"Go, and put to death all those Fathers." The command being given—the sentence being pronounced—there could be no mistake regarding the issue. No repeal, no change, was to be expected ; so the Governor went silently to execute the awful deed. But, on the evening before, after the sitting of the Council, it had already transpired that the sentence was pronounced against the Christians in Japan. The news spread with the rapidity of lightning through all the country, and this recently imported Christianity presented one of the most wonderful spectacles ever witnessed in the Church of God. Every one disposed of his goods. There were mutual felicitations and congratulations interchanged amongst the Christians, and they invited each other to festive gatherings. They rejoiced exceedingly that now they were on the eve of the glorious day, on which through blood they would leave earth and be transplanted into Paradise. They purchased new garments to wear upon their great festal day. All wished to die for Jesus Christ, and their only fear was that they should escape notice and be deprived of the glorious palm and trophy of martyrdom. On the 12th December, the sentence was communicated to the Fathers, whose joy was now unbounded. The edict of the Emperor included " all the Fathers."* The Governor was now beset with two difficulties :—firstly, he was in doubt whether the decree included the Jesuits or not. After some discussion on that point, the Emperor consented to leave them free, with the exception of a few who had been too zealous in propagating the new doctrine, and had dared to resist his orders, which had forbidden them to preach in public and to

---

* The word "Fathers" was meant to signify not only the Religious, but all who had any connexion with them.

baptize the converted Japanese. He had issued this decree, he said, because under the *false* pretext that they must " *obey God rather than men*," they had dared, by preaching and other means, to labour to plant their new doctrines on the ruins of the ancient religion of the country. " I, therefore, order," said he, " these to be executed; the others who have so far obeyed my orders must be left in peace for a little while." The second difficulty which created doubt in the mind of Gibonoshio was whether the decree included the Fathers who came with the galleon. When the Minister proposed this doubt, the Emperor was seized with fury, and he promptly and in great wrath exclaimed : — " They more than the others have merited to die, because their object has manifestly been acknowledged." It appears that the Governor ventured to make some remarks upon the inaccuracies of the pilot's statements which had given excuse for the passing of this decree, for, as he observed, all the rest, including the Religious, who had come in the ship had disclaimed against the charges made, and had solemnly protested that no such intentions had been entertained by them ; and he himself (the Governor) was bound, he said, to say that he could not believe it, because all the Christians had shown themselves as dutiful and loyal to the Emperor and his Government, and had never given any just cause for suspicion. But Taiko-Sama, being entirely blinded by his headstrong passions, was unable to understand the force of the Governor's reasoning; so he severely rebuked his Minister, and peremptorily commanded that his decree should be duly executed. There was now no hope left : the sunshine of prosperity was to be succeeded by the gloom of adversity, and mild toleration was to be taken away to give place for savage persecution. Gibonoshio, through motives of humanity, had thus far done his best; but his reasoning, though solid and conclusive, was unheeded, and, as a servant, he was compelled to obey his master. It is painful to see men endowed with good qualities, both of the head and heart, obliged by official ties, not only to connive at, but to participate in the crimes and injustice of their cruel and despotic masters. They are conscious that in too many instances the commands imposed are iniquitous, but they have neither virtue enough to protest against the iniquity, nor disinterestedness enough to throw up office, sooner than act against their convictions. Alas! how deceitful is the world! how cruel and unjust! From the very foundation of kingdoms to the present time, State chicanery has allied itself with every thing that was monopolising, selfish, mean, and demoralising. In Pagan times men were left groping in the dark, for the light of revelation did not illumine their minds, neither did its moral code regulate their lives. But, why feel surprise? The world has, during eighteen centuries, been brilliantly lit up by the glittering beams of the Sun of Evangelical Truth, and Emperors and Kings, with their Ministers, have been basking beneath the rays of that glorious orb; yet who can recount the miseries which have been inflicted upon the human family by the united efforts of kingly ambition and ministerial subserviency? Who is there so skilled in figures as to be able to enumerate the robberies perpetrated on the poor—the murders committed on the innocent—the crimes imputed to the guileless—the outrages inflicted on the Church—the blasphemies poured out against God—and the millions of souls sent into eternal perdition—through means of this nefarious combination? Now, if those things have happened in the world from the time that Kings became Christians, and do happen in our own days, why should we be amazed at finding that amongst Pagans such men as Gibonoshio should, contrary to their convictions, aid tyranny in its persecution of truth and innocence? Perhaps we are asking too much of poor human nature, particularly under the present circumstances; and we must not lose sight of the fact that Gibonoshio was still moping in the darkness of Paganism, and guided by the dim and flickering light of unassisted reason. He could not understand that the law of the living and only true God, based upon the principles of eternal justice, was to take precedence of all human laws—that God was to be preferred to men; neither could he, by the mere dint of ratiocination, account for the motives which had induced the Christians to make such noble and generous sacrifices. It was God's prevenient grace, with which they heartily co-operated, that had infused the habit and had perfected its growth. He was a stranger to its influence, and perverted human reason—his only guide—led him into fatal error. His good qualities were the products of human helps, whose foundations are based upon quicksands; and he failed to comprehend rightly and to act wisely, because mere human virtues are unentitled to supernatural rewards. In God we live, and move, and exist; by His grace we can do all things, but without it we are weak, and faltering, and impotent.

The Governor, thus instructed by the Emperor, sent immediate orders to Nangazaki, which was under the governorship of a certain man named Tarazava. In the writ forwarded to Tarazava, he was informed that in a few days the Franciscan Fathers should arrive, and that they should be crucified near the town of Nangazaki. Tarazava, without delay, commissioned Fazamburo to prepare all the necessaries for the execution of the Emperor's decree.

The Spanish crew of the galleon, being made acquainted with the Emperor's decree, were plunged into deep affliction, and above all the rest the unfortunate pilot, the ill-fated author of all the uproar. He laboured, but fruitlessly, to recall his words. His counter-protestations were unheeded, for the fire had been enkindled, and it must now burn until all is consumed. The Spaniards, in order to solace their souls and obtain comfort in their afflictions, asked their guards to grant them permission to visit Father Martinus de Aguirre, at Osaka, that they might have the very pleasing satisfaction to make their confessions to a future martyr. The permission was granted, but under the condition to bring back with them Father Joannes de Zamorra. The holy man was so overwhelmed with grief, that he wept very bitterly to see that the palm of martyrdom would not be given to him, but was to be unfortunately snatched from his grasp. The good Fathers Rodrigues, Ribadinrerio, and Ruiz were shut up in another ship, and orders were given to send them out of the country; but Father Zamorra, still clinging to the hope of being martyred, walked publicly through the streets of the town, clothed in his Habit, in order that the authorities might take hold of him, and, eventually, lead him to the acquisition of a martyr's crown. He, however, laboured in vain. Day after day succeeded each other, and the Father was constantly seen wandering about, like a strayed sheep, to find a place amongst the fortunate number of his blessed brethren. He sought for death, and death fled from him. He was a very zealous and holy man; he had predicted many eventful things, and they came to pass. He had been in Japan before, but Father Petrus Baptista sent him to the Philippine Islands to transact important business, and he had just returned to Japan. Who could have doubted but he was destined for the crown of martyrdom? But no! though he was taken prisoner with the Fathers at Osaka, he was not reckoned amongst the proscribed Missionaries, because he had arrived in the galleon. The blessed Philippus, who had arrived in the same vessel, was taken prisoner; and though he had never been in Japan before, had never preached, had not as yet laboured publicly on the Japanese soil, yet he obtained the crown of martyrdom. Must we not then exclaim with the Apostle of the Gentiles, Romans xi. 33 — "*How incomprehensible are His judgments, and how unsearchable His ways!* in which He (God) leads his elect to glory." When blessed Philippus saw all his Brethren bound with chains, he exclaimed with great enthusiasm :— "Far be it from me that I should go free, when all my Brethren are in chains. I will share in all their sufferings." He had scarcely uttered these words when he was arrested, and he, too, was reckoned with the other Fathers. But the saintly Brother Joannes de Zamorra, whatever he did, however perseveringly he begged to be reckoned amongst them, could not obtain the grand object of his desires. He went several times to the Governor and to the guards, and offered himself as a victim for the approaching sacrifice; but he was every time met by refusal, and then he burst out into tears at losing the prospect of wearing a martyr's crown. He was now carefully watched by the guards, that he might be brought back to the Spanish ship, with the other Spaniards, who soon returned to Macao, where they were obliged to remain until they should be sent home to Spain. When they arrived at the first stage of their journey from Nangazaki, they met the Sub-governor, Fazamburo, who was to superintend the cruel decree of the Emperor, which commanded the holy Martyrs to be crucified. Fazamburo said he had orders from the Emperor to provide Father Joannes and his companions with all necessaries, but the holy man did not desire anything but the crown of martyrdom. They passed the night about three miles from Nangazaki; but at midnight a great noise was heard, and there was a rush made to the door. The Fathers, who had been conducted on shipboard, had then arrived. All the people in the house were ordered away, and none of the Spanish crew were allowed to speak to the holy martyrs. Brother Joannes de Zamorra now secretly rejoiced, for he fondly thought that the long-desired moment had arrived in which he would be permitted to join his fortunate Brothers. He escaped the notice of the guards who were appointed to watch him, and he endeavoured to place himself amongst the martyrs; but Fazamburo noticed him, and ordering him back, said:—" Go away; you do not belong to this brotherhood : I have orders to crucify them after the space of one hour." Father Joannes replied :—" Yes, I do belong to them ; if you put them to death because they have preached, I have done the same, and therefore I deserve the same punishment." In answer to this, Fazamburo said:—" I know and see very well that you are at least their companion, but I will not put you to death; and, if it were in my power, I would release those marked out for execution." Fazamburo finding that words were thrown away upon the Brother Joannes, ordered his hands to be tied behind his back, and he sent him under the charge of four soldiers to the Spanish crew. The soldiers received strict orders to watch him very closely, that he might be securely conveyed to Miako, with four others. Brother Joannes, seeing that all hope of receiving the palm was lost to him, wept so bitterly, and lamented so piteously, that he moved every one to tears. The holy man's eyes were constantly turned towards his fortunate Brethren, who were so soon to be translated into the heavenly kingdom.

The Martyrs then remained at Miako during the month of December, in charge of a guard of soldiers. They had to endure great hardships from the brutality of the soldiers, and also from the want of all things. But they considered their inability to assist the poor forlorn Christians, and more especially the sick and miserable in the hospitals, to be their greatest calamity. They constantly prayed that God would supply the wants of this new Mission at that moment of such severe trials. Holy Petrus Baptista sent letters to Jerome de Jesu, beseeching him to conceal himself that he might thus be enabled to give, secretly, assistance and consolation to the Christians, and encouragement and strength to bear their sufferings with patience and resignation.

In the mean time, the Governor of Miako ordered all the names to be taken of the Christians who had had any communication with the Franciscan Fathers. When the number of such was found to be amazingly great, he said that he only meant those amongst them who had been in close relations with them ; but even this number was found to be too large ; therefore he ordered a few to be called, and he asked them whether they had had any close connexion with the Franciscan Brothers. Those who answered affirmatively were requested by him to sign their names. All were willing to have their names inscribed on the paper, but those who were unable to write were commanded to stand back. Nevertheless, the list soon became too large, and, therefore, the Governor selected only twelve for execution. He endeavoured to persuade the Emperor not to put the condemned to death, but to send them into banishment ; but the blood-thirsty Jacuinus interfered, and pressed harder than ever upon Taiko-Sama to have his decrees respected and faithfully and punctually put into execution. The Emperor, thus constantly pressed

and excited by this impious man, and falling again
into one of those terrible paroxysms of anger to which
he was subjected, ordered that the ears and noses of
the condemned should be cut off; that in that
mutilated state they should be carried about the
chief town of his dominions, and afterwards crucified
at Nangazaki. This decree was final.

Whilst the Fathers were singing Vespers, three
officers with a body of soldiers approached the Convent. When the holy men heard the noise and saw
the rush at the door of the Convent, they were firmly
convinced that the happy hour had struck. Father
Petrus Baptista, the Superior, took the Cross on
which was nailed the figure of our Crucified Lord
and reverently kissed the feet, and as a good shepherd put himself at the head of his Brethren, to meet
with joy and cheerfulness those cruel barbarians that
were sent to torture them and then to put them to
death. They marched in solemn procession, chanting
as they walked along the rest of the Vespers. They
never ceased praising and blessing God. The soldiers
immediately bound the Fathers amidst a crowd of
eager spectators, who were watching with indiscribable
sorrow the cruel proceedings, and whose loud lamentations, sobs, and sighs were heartrending. When
the binding was finished, their names were called out,-
and the Brother-Cook, Matthias, was found absent
(he had been sent, with one soldier to guard him,
about some commission into the town); the officer
cried out, "Where is Matthias? Does any one
know where he is? The list must be complete,
where is he? Tell us where he is?" As they were
searching for him, and calling him by name, a
Christian, who was a good friend to the Fathers,
stepped boldly forward and said: "Here is Matthias,
my name is Matthias, if not the one you seek, at
least one who glories in having the same feelings."

The officers said : "That will do." He was bound and put with the others. The holy man, finding himself again in the company of his best friends, shed tears of joy because God would bestow upon him the exceedingly great blessing of dying a martyr for the truth of the doctrines taught by His own Infallible Church; a favour which he had long and earnestly petitioned for.

All the Christians, and those who had visited the Fathers, were deprived of all their goods. The Martyrs were stripped of their clothes, except the underdress; and the wives and children of those who were married amongst the prisoners were carried to Pagan houses.

As we have seen above, the Emperor's decree did not include all the Jesuits, but only a few. Three were taken prisoners at Osaka, namely, Paulus Michi, Jacobus Kisai, and Joannes Goto. Some of the officers were inclined to liberate Paulus Michi, but the holy man, who was a nobleman by birth but more noble by virtue, courageously answered that he would follow Jesus Christ to death, and that he would not separate himself from the holy children of St. Francis, for whom he always had a peculiar devotion, the zeal of whose children he had always admired and had endeavoured to copy; and that he esteemed himself only too happy to suffer with them. Thus God gave to the Illustrious Society, which had laid the foundation of the true faith in Japan, the honour of counting some of its members amongst the first Martyrs.

CHAPTER XI.

IN one of the preceding chapters we gave a short
legend of the following Fathers:—Petrus Baptista,
Martinus de Aguirre, Francis Blanco, Philippus a Jesu,
Gonsalvus Garcia, and Francis of St. Michael. All
these belonged to the first Order of St. Francis of
Assisium. We will now give the names of the others,
that our readers may have all the names in vivid
recollection: we will add a short legend of each,
based upon such evidence as we have been able to
collect respecting them. The following seventeen
were of the third Order of St. Francis, and the three
last belonged to the Society of Jesus.*

1. Cosmas Tachegia. He was born in the small
kingdom of Oaris, in Japan. His occupation in the
world was that of sharpening swords. His disposition was exceedingly mild; he had only very recently
been baptized, and he led a most holy life. His constant aim was to labour by prayer, and the punctual

---

* It appears that it was originally intended to Canonise the twenty-
three Franciscan Martyrs, who suffered death in Japan, and with them
the holy Confessor, B. Michael de Sanctis, of the renowned Order of
the Holy Trinity for the Redemption of Captives. But we now find
that the three Martyrs of the Order of the Society of Jesus, who were
crucified with the Franciscans, were also Canonised on Whit-Sunday.
The number of Saints then Canonised was twenty-seven, viz., twenty-
six Martyrs, and one Confessor.

observance of the divine law to preserve his baptismal innocence unsullied. He was the companion of Father Martinus, and he acted as his interpreter. He was glad to suffer with the other Fathers, and he looked upon the Cross with delight, believing that it would be instrumental in taking him to heaven ; that it would be the key to unlock its gates to admit him into the society of the blessed, where his sufferings would be eternally rewarded with the fruition of its ineffable delights. His Cross was the second on the eastern side.

2. Michael Cosacki.. He was born in the kingdom of Isk, in Japan. He lived in the vicinity of the Convent of the Franciscan Fathers, and he was by trade a manufacturer of arrows. He was the father of Thomas Cosacki, one of those three admirable children whom we shall soon have an opportunity of introducing to the notice of our readers. Through a singular coincidence this happy father had the plea-sure of seeing his fortunate child obtain, at the same time with himself, the glorious crown of martyrdom, and thus hand in hand they entered the eternal kingdom. Their Crosses did not stand close to each other; the Cross of Michael Cosacki was the fourth on the eastern side. Michael had always been very sincerely devoted to the Franciscan Fathers, whose zeal he admired. He was foremost amongst all the seventeen by the firmness of his faith ; he was strictly upright in his dealings ; he was extremely charitable, and after his work was finished he was accustomed to visit the hospitals and attend upon the sick and miserable, and his own house was always open to the needy and the wayfarer.

3. Cajus Franciscus. The place of his birth is unknown. We, at least, after a very careful investi-gation, have not been able to discover it. He was by trade a carpenter, had been received into the Church

about eight months before his martyrdom, and had very recently received the Sacrament of Confirmation. As soon as he heard that the Franciscan Fathers had been arrested, he courageously offered himself to the officers and soldiers, and told them that he too was a Christian, and a great friend of the Fathers. He visited the holy prisoners, and when they were brought through the streets of Miako, and exposed to the mockery of the mob, Cajus joined himself to them in order to share in the ignominy. The soldiers endeavoured in vain to drive him away from the waggon ; they beat him violently, and then dragged him off; but he clung so closely to it that they could not remove him, and thus he promenaded the city with the holy prisoners. This promenading was considered by the Emperor as an act that would cast reproach upon the servants of Christ; but they rejoiced at this display of Imperial malignity, and looked upon it as a glorious triumph for religion, and as a spectacle that would fill the holy Angels with joy. Cajus was attentive to the prisoners throughout the journey, and was anxiously desirous of obtaining the crown of martyrdom. He constantly returned to the Martyrs, was frequently beaten with much cruelty, but he always returned with the same indomitable courage. The very Pagans themselves were compelled to admire such wonderful courage and charity as were exhibited by the Christians. Taiko-Sama himself, having been informed of this incident, exclaimed :— " How courageous these Christians are ! and how closely and intimately they are united ! Oh ! how ardently they love one another !" At last, Cajus obtained the object of all his desires ; what he had perseveringly prayed for was now within his grasp; he was aggregated to the holy band of Martyrs, and was crucified. His Cross was the first on the east of the hill, on which the crucifixion took place.

4. Petrus Suchegiro. His birthplace is not known, neither has it been ascertained what was his trade or calling in the world. He was a most zealous friend of the Fathers of the Society of Jesus, and, finding that the Martyrs were going to be crucified at Nangazaki, he took measures for providing the Franciscan Fathers with all requisites during their painful journey. The Christians were well acquainted with the zeal and courage of Petrus, and they therefore chose him to perform this work of charity towards the Martyrs. Petrus was only too glad to have so favourable an opportunity of exhibiting his faith and charity. He, moreover, thought that this was a favourable occasion for getting the palm of martyrdom. He, like Cajus Franciscus, took every opportunity of showing himself with the Martyrs. At length the officers and soldiers, tired of rebuking him, placed him with the martyrs, and he was crucified. He was fastened to the third Cross on the eastern side. He lovingly embraced the instrument of his martyrdom, and kissed the blessed wood; whilst his cheeks were suffused with tears and his heart was overflowing with joy.

5. Paulus Ibarki. He was a native of the small Princedom of Oasis, and had only recently been baptised. He was constantly with the Fathers and served on many occasions as interpreter for them. His Cross stood between those of Paulus Michi and Joannes Goto, two of the Jesuit Fathers. He died with a cheerful countenance.

6. Lewis. This child was only ten years of age. He had been instructed in the Christian faith by the Franciscan Fathers : he served at the altar. When the list of the Martyrs was made up, Lewis was rejected; but he cried so bitterly and entreated the officers so forcibly, that he obtained the favour of having his name enrolled amongst the rest. Whilst

confined in prison, a Pagan of great consideration in
the town went over to see Lewis, and he promised to
procure his liberation if he would renounce his faith
and return to the worship of the idols. The saintly
youth courageously replied: "It is you who must
become a Christian, for there is no other way to save
your soul." The seducer returned ashamed and
astonished to find such firmness in a child of such
tender years. The decree of Taiko-Sama ordered
that the Martyrs should lose their ears and noses by
amputation, but the officers were satisfied with cutting
off a piece of the left ear. The child suffered this
first effusion of blood with wonderful courage and joy.
When the Martyrs were thrown into a cart to be
drawn through the streets, all eyes were directed
towards those three little children that formed a part
of the band, and especially towards Lewis, whose
countenance was bright with joy, and who, with an
angelic voice, sang the Pater Noster, the Ave Maria,
and other devout prayers. The crowds of people who
were present were unable to master their emotions,
and they burst out into sobs and tears.

When the Martyrs arrived at Carazu, on their
way to Nangazaki, they were met by Fazamburo.
This official had been acquainted with Paulus Michi,
and he endeavoured to seduce him; but being
unable to succeed, he turned his attention towards
Lewis, and, moved with compassion, he said: "My
dear child, your life is in my hands, if you agree to
serve me, I will deliver you." The child answered:
"I do not decide anything on my own account; I
will do what Petrus Baptista will decide for me." The
blessed Petrus Baptista at once replied to Fazamburo,
by saying: "He accepts your offer on one condition,
viz., that he be allowed to remain a *Christian*." Upon
this the Sub-Governor said: "No; he must renounce
the Christian doctrine." Then little Lewis answered

without the least hesitation, " Upon this condition I do not wish to live; for this miserable and short life, I will not sacrifice an eternity of happiness."

As soon as the party reached the place of execution, and Lewis knew which Cross was his, he leaped over it with inexpressible joy and delight. When fixed to the cross, he expressed his joy by the movement of his eyes and fingers, and by the brightness of his countenance. The Martyrs intoned with angelic voices the Psalm, " *Laudate pueri Dominum*," "*Praise the Lord ye children*,"—and when they had come to the Doxology, the lances of the soldiers pierced their breasts and hearts, and they finished the Psalm with the Angels above.

7. Anthony. He was a child of only twelve years of age; he was born at Nangazaki. He had a most excellent disposition, and he was singularly amiable and gentle in his manners. The holy Petrus Baptista loved him with great affection. · Anthony served him at the altar and was the companion of little Lewis. He could have easily escaped the punishment of death, but, like his companion, he resolved not to abandon the Fathers, if even death were awarded as the recompense of his devoted attachment. Anthony and Lewis were taken prisoners at the same time, their hands were tied behind their backs, and they were placed at the head of the others. A terrible struggle awaited him at Nangazaki, where his father and mother resided. Both were Christians, and they rejoiced with their whole hearts at finding that their holy child, of such tender years, was deemed by God worthy of dying a martyr's death. But, on the other hand, overcome by the natural feelings of parents, they went to the place of execution, and whilst a copious stream of tears rolled down their cheeks, they besought the meek and courageous Anthony not to give himself up to death in the very

H

commencement of youth; and they told him that he would afterwards have many occasions of showing his zeal for religion. The admirable boy, interiorly strengthened by God's grace, resisted this first assault, and he very courageously said to his parents : " Do not trouble yourselves about me, for I have a firm confidence that God will assist me to the very end. And as far as you yourselves are concerned, let me beg of you not to cry, not to weep, not even to sigh for me. Cease to expose your want of faith to the scorn of those surrounding Pagans." The parents insisted with greater force, and the Sub-Governor, seeing that they could not prevail upon Anthony, stepped forward and. said : " My child, do not resist your parents ; obey them, and I will take care of you. I promise you great favours from Taiko-Sama." " And for whom," replied the child, " will those favours be ? Shall I be allowed to share them with these Fathers?" " No,' said Fazamburo, " they will be for yourself only." " Then," answered the heroic Anthony, "keep them for yourself, for our Lord, who is above, has greater and more lasting favours for me and these good Fathers, above in heaven ; we shall share them there together. I do not fear death ; I love the Cross." Having spoken thus to the Sub-Governor, he bid farewell to his parents, and promising to pray for them in heaven, he again besought them not to cry for him, but for the blind Pagans, who were sitting in the darkness, and corrupted by the abominations of idolatry. His Cross stood near that of Father Petrus Baptista ; as soon, therefore, as he was fastened to it, he invited the good Father to sing with him the Psalm " *Laudate pueri Dominum.*" But Father Petrus Baptista was wrapt in silent and ecstatic prayer, and gave no answer ; and the child then began the Psalm with Lewis, and received at the same moment the death-blow from the spear that pierced his tender heart. Oh! holy child, may we join with you in the choirs of heaven, and sing in concert the sweet praises of our good and loving God!

8. Thomas Cosacki. He was the son of Michael Cosacki, and was a child of only twelve years of age. He showed to the very end a remarkable degree of courage ; the same cheerfulness and joyfulness, which distinguished the little Lewis and Anthony were conspicuous in him, and these things caused the very heathens to admire their conduct, and to be stupefied at the occurrence of such strange events. They could not understand how such tender children could be possessed of such amazing courage and fortitude in the presence of so ignominious a death.

9. Mathias. He was the person who was substituted for Mathias the Cook, who was absent about business when the others were arrested. His name had been on the list from the beginning, and he had been one of the first who offered themselves ; but it was struck off, and he became very sorrowful because he thought that he was about to lose such a favourable opportunity of entering into the glory of heaven. God, however, arranged matters in his favour, and by the occurrence of the absence of Mathias, the Cook, he obtained the happy accomplishment of all his desires. He persevered in prayer until his heart was pierced.

10. Leo Carasuma. He was by birth a Japanese; he was the brother of Paulus Ibarki and the uncle of little Lewis. He instructed the children and the neophytes in the Christian doctrine, and zealously prepared them for the worthy participation of the Holy Sacraments : he also frequently acted as interpreter for the Fathers, He was greatly admired for the charity with which he served the sick and miserable in the hospitals. His temper was sweet and compassionate, and he was greatly beloved by

every one. He unceasingly thanked God with great earnestness for having bestowed upon him the great grace of martyrdom, and when his heart was pierced by the lance he was engaged in singing with the three children the praises of the Lord.

11. Bonaventura. He was born in Japan of Christian parents, who died when he was young, He had been brought up a Pagan and had lost the faith he had received in baptism. But, on remembering that he ought to profess the Christian religion, he felt himself interiorly moved ; he went to the Franciscan Fathers, who kindly instructed him in the true faith. He renounced his errors, and was very sincere and zealous in the practice of the observances of religion. He would never leave his dear Fathers, and he served them with great fidelity and courage. He was one of the first whose names were placed upon the list. His soul was inebriated with delight when he found that he was deemed worthy to shed his blood for Jesus Christ—his loving master—and with much serenity and cheerfulness he received the wound which pierced his purified heart and sent his soul to Paradise.

12. Joachim Saccachibara. He was a native of Japan, and was born at Osaka. From the very beginning he had zealously devoted himself to the services of the Fathers. He had some knowledge of medicine, and was very useful in the hospitals; and in them he served the sick with much devotedness and charity. He was forty years of age when he received the martyr's crown.

13. Franciscus of Miako. He was born at Miako, in Japan, and he was a very skilful physician. He devoted himself entirely to the Fathers, assisting them in their labours, instructing the people, and acting as interpreter for those amongst them who could not express themselves with sufficient clearness

in the Japanese language. It seems that he wrote a few treatises to refute the absurdities and to remove the prejudices of the Japanese people.

14. Thomas Danchi. He was also born at Miako, of Japanese parents. He, too, was in the service of the Fathers, was a good interpreter, and served with great assiduity in the hospitals. He deemed it a very great honour to be numbered with the Martyrs, and to deserve so easily the crown of glory. He thanked God and cheerfully embraced his Cross.

15. John Chimoia. He, too, was born at Miako. He was only very recently baptized, and he only joined the Third Order of St. Francis a few days before his capture; and, though he only came at the eleventh hour, he received the same reward as the others.

16. Gabriel. He was born in the kingdom of Isk, in Japan, and he resided with the Fathers as a student. He was only nineteen years of age when he was taken prisoner, and he rejoiced because he was deemed worthy to die the death of a Martyr for the Lord Jesus Christ.

17. Paulus Suzuchi. He was born in the kingdom of Oaris, in Japan. He wrote several tracts for the instruction of the neophytes. He was the principal Catechist, and he devoted all his leisure hours to attendance on the the sick in the hospitals. He was delighted at finding that God had selected him as one of the chosen band who were to seal their religious convictions with their blood. His Cross was the last on the western side of the hill.

All these, seventeen in number, were laymen belonging to the Third Order of St. Francis; into which they had been received not long before they were taken prisoners.

The three following belonged to the glorious Order of the Society of Jesus, whose members had so faithfully laboured for the conversion of Japan. It was just that their blood should be commingled with that of the children of St. Francis. They had worked together—they had the same holy end constantly in view; and if accidental differences may have arisen as to the means to be employed, and the time and manner in which they should be employed, they never doubted of each other's intentions. Their hearts were united; and a reciprocity of feeling and an identity of interest kept them bound together with the cords of fraternal love. The first, or chief, of the three Fathers of the Society of Jesus, who suffered martyrdom, was—

1. Paulus Michi. He was a Japanese by birth, and even some historians assert that he was descended from a noble family. He was once a distinguished officer, and by his superior qualities he rendered himself a great favourite at the Court of the Emperor Nobununga. He became a Christian in 1568. He entered the Society of Jesus in 1586, and he made great progress in the spiritual life and in his theological studies. He was also one of the most important preachers in Japan; and it was on account of his great and ardent zeal that he was numbered amongst the Franciscan Fathers, for whom he had always felt a peculiar affection. Having received from God the grace of the apostleship, he could not see how any human power should interfere with his zeal. God moved him (he inwardly felt), he must then follow the motion and the direction of God; and fearless of death, under whatever shape it might present itself, he must evangelise. When a prisoner and bound with chains, he preached to the people whenever he saw them. Thrown amongst criminals condemned for their crimes, he preached to them the salutary doctrine of Christianity. When removed from one place to another he preached, now to the

soldiers, now to the people; and at other times he encouraged his Brothers in chains. When fixed upon his Cross he declared, once for all, that there was no other road to heaven than that which the Christian religion pointed out. He cheerfully forgave his enemies, and those who had condemned him to death; conjuring them with his last breath to become Christians. Having finished his discourse, and seeing the soldier approaching with his spear, he said : "Oh ! Lord, into Thy hands I commend my spirit;" and then received the stroke of death.

2. Joannes Goto. He was born of Christian parents in the Island of Goto. He had devoted himself early in life to the service of the Jesuit Missionaries, assisting them at the altar and acting as catechist. He was taken prisoner, and condemned on account of his zeal in propagating the Christian religion. When he arrived at the place of execution, he gave his beads to his father, and to his mother he gave the handkerchief which had been wrapped about his head. He died a cheerful death. His father stood under the Cross, and received on his clothes the blood of his martyred son, and then, kissing the Cross, he withdrew.

3. Jacobus Kisai. He was a native of the Kingdom of Bigen, in Japan. He had been married, but his wife having apostatised, he left her, and placed his child in a good Christian school. He retired from the world, and entered the Society of Jesus, at Osaka. Being well instructed in religion, he was frequently employed as catechist. He was a man of prayer, and spent the greater part of the day in the contemplation of the Passion of our Lord—his special object of devotion. When he was taken prisoner, all the people took great compassion upon him, on account of his great age. Some showed public sympathy for him, but he humbly answered: "I am a

great sinner." When he was fixed upon the Cross, his lips were constantly moving in prayer, and his last words were "Jesus, Maria;" and, finally, he resigned his soul, enriched with virtue in a supereminent degree, into the hands of his Saviour.

We have now given a brief sketch of each Martyr in particular, as far as history has supplied the materials. They were twenty-six in number who found themselves united together in the common prison, at Miako. They were united in faith and in sufferings, and they were all simultaneously pierced with lances, and received their crowns together. May they unitedly pray for the salvation of those who read their legends, and for the whole world.

CHAPTER XII.

HAVING given in the foregoing chapters a short legend of each of the Martyrs through their several sufferings, we now hasten to give more particulars of what further occurred previously to their execution. Our readers will remember that we have already stated, that it was whilst the Martyrs at Miako were singing Vespers, they were apprehended. They continued the Vespers during the painful operation of having their hands tied behind their backs. When this was completed, the Martyrs, with a cheerful voice, intoned the beautiful song—" *Te Deum Laudamus,*" " *We praise the Lord,*" but, before they could finish it, they were compelled by force to leave the Church. The crowd of people which had assembled together was, however, so great, that they could not be marched out as quickly as the soldiers desired. This circumstance was seized hold of by the Fathers, and thus they had ample time for finishing the chant of that splendid hymn. Before they reached the vestibule of the Convent, they passed once more the door of the Church, and, pausing for a moment, they intoned the " *Gloriosa Domina,*" " *O Glorious Lady,*" in honour of the Blessed Virgin, the peculiar Patroness of that Church : they then parted for ever

with that sacred Sanctuary, endeared to them by so
many titles It was there, during the period of four
years, that they had witnessed so many prodigies. It
was there they had found grace to sanctify themselves,
and celestial aid to convert the sinner. Passing the
door of the hospital, in which there lay so many unfortunate sufferers, whom they had loved so tenderly,
and had served so faithfully, so charitably, so kindly,
and who were now thrown into the ruthless and
merciless hands of Pagans and barbarians, the
Martyrs were deeply affected when they contemplated
this state of things—bursting into tears they wept
bitterly. Some of the poor sick creatures left their
beds and looked through the windows, to take a last
parting glance at their kind benefactors, their true
and devoted friends. Those broken-hearted people
howled and shouted as loudly as their infirmities
would permit, in order to express their sympathy for
the Martyrs, so cruelly, so iniquitously dragged along,
having their hands, which had only been used in
conferring blessings and favours, so rudely tied behind
their backs. When the Fathers beheld those miserable lepers, they fervently prayed to God in their
behalf, and sent them their last blessing. The
soldiers, obeying the orders of their officers, pressed
on more quickly, for general sympathy was more and
more manifesting itself amongst the constantly increasing crowds, which formed an immense procession around the Martyrs. The crowds were not
composed of Christians only, but of Pagans too,
whose number exceeded that of the Christians.
The Pagans themselves, following the natural ten-
dency of their characteristic feelings, could not avoid
now and then uttering a sob or a sigh for those innocent victims. The Bonzes were busily employed
amongst the crowds in striving to check the exhibi-
tion of such sympathy, and to replace it by vociferous

shouts and false accusations against the holy Missionaries. But they greatly failed in their endeavours, as was soon seen; for from the corners of all the streets fresh manifestations arose in favour of the Martyrs. The people even threw themselves at the feet of the holy prisoners, kissed them reverently, and they also kissed the hem of their garments; and, not being yet satisfied, they kissed the very marks of their footsteps. The old and faithful Joya*, the Syndic of the Convent, followed the Fathers all the way; and, when they approached the common prison, he became so much excited that, in spite of the soldiers, he threw his arms around the neck of one of the Fathers and embraced him most tenderly, weeping bitterly because he was not permitted to be one of their glorious company. One of the soldiers, unable to loose his hands clasped around the Father, gave him so severe a blow upon the face that he fell to the ground, which he kissed devoutly; at the same time he returned hearty thanks to God, because for His sake he had at least suffered something. His loving heart turned to Jesus his Saviour; and, thankful for all His mercies, he besought Him that he might obtain the death of the just. His wife Maria showed the same zeal; and, though the soldiers beat her very severely, they could not drive her away. At last they bound her, and sent her home with a small guard. At length they arrived at Miako, and were lodged in the common prison: it was the 30th day of December. The Emperor gave orders that the Martyrs from Osaka should be brought to Miako, together with the three Fathers of the Society of Jesus. The number now amounted to twenty-four: two others subsequently joined them on the road to Nangazaki; and thus the full number of twenty-six was completed

---

* The person appointed to superintend the temporal affairs of the Convent.

Who could describe the rapture of joy they felt, when they saw each other after so long an absence? With much warmth of affection, many felicitations and congratulations were interchanged between them. The very soldiers were moved. The Martyrs knelt down together, and thanked God for the great favour he had bestowed upon them. They comforted each other, but no encouragement was needed; for their zeal was already very great, and their readiness for martyrdom was exceedingly prompt. They were bound, and shut up in a narrow, unhealthy dungeon; but the Word of God was not bound. They preached to the people from the openings of the prison, and animated the Christians by their fervid discourses to perseverance; and they invited the Pagans to become converted to the true religion of Jesus Christ, who lovingly died for the salvation of all mankind. One of the Judges, surprised at such staunch and persevering zeal, asked Father Petrus Baptista why so many Christians wished to be martyred? The holy man cheerfully answered :— " Because it is so easy a way to go to heaven, and so cheap a price to buy the eternal goods !" This answer pleased the Judge, who said that he also wished to become a Christian, and liked to hear their doctrine.

On the evening of the 2nd of January, they were informed that on the next day their martyrdom would begin. They spent the whole night in prayer and in praising God. On the 3rd of January they were in reality brought out of the prison, with their hands tied behind their backs, and were then dragged through the principal streets of Miako, until they arrived at the great public place, in front of the principal Temple of the Idols. The decree of Taiko-Sama condemned each of them to lose both ears and the nose; but the Governor, Gibonoshio, was satisfied with cutting off only a piece of the left ear. Great was the joy of the holy company when they suffered this first effusion of their blood; and this joy was increased by the reflection that the Church at that time remembered and commemorated in her divine office the first effusion of our Blessed Saviour's blood, by the instrument of circumcision. It seems rather astonishing that Gibonoshio dared to make so great an alteration in the Emperor's decree; and it can only be accounted for by assuming that to be true which was currently rumoured, namely—that he felt a secret compassion for the Martyrs, and even a strong leaning towards their doctrine. Some historians also remark that a great and very influential Prince of Japan had said that it was both unbecoming and unjust in the great Japanese nation to sacrifice those innocent men. Whether it be true or not, it is certain that the Emperor's decree was only partially executed, and we do not find that Taiko-Sama ever censured Gibonoshio for his apparent indulgence.

When the painful operation was accomplished, the Christians gathered as *souvenirs,* or relicts, those pieces of the Martyrs' ears, and conserved them with great care.

Eight cars, or waggons, were now brought to the spot, and the Martyrs were commanded to mount upon them. Each waggon was to carry three. This manner of conveyance was looked upon by the Japanese as the greatest disgrace. The waggons were drawn along by oxen.

In front of one of the carts there was carried on a high peak the following inscription : " Because these men, having come as ambassadors into Japan, have preached, contrary to my orders, the Christian religion, I order that they shall be put to death. Consequently, those twenty-four shall be crucified at Nangazaki. And, that every one should know my will, I hereby do again forbid to propagate in Japan and in the whole of my dominions the Christian doctrine ; and should any one dare to transgress this decree, he and his whole family and tribe shall be exterminated."

On the first waggon was seated Petrus Baptista, the chief and leader of them all. He had the Cross which he had brought from the Convent with him, hanging on his breast, because his hands being bound behind his back he could not carry it in them. He turned himself with his breast to the Fathers, that they all might see the Cross, and remember the death of their Lord and Redeemer. The crowd of people was immense, and the commotion was indescribable. The streets were choked up, the windows were filled, the roofs of the houses were covered along all the streets through which the Martyrs had to pass. The citizens, both Christians and Pagans, had cleansed all the streets, and covered them with ashes, a ceremony, if it may be called such, which is never performed in Japan, except for solemn processions in honour of Emperors, or Kings, or some other exalted personages worthy of peculiar honour. The soldiers, guards, officers, and judges were busily occupied in clearing the way for the passage of the waggons. The Martyrs seated in them were so cheerful, their countenances were beaming with such delight that the promenade, which was intended for an affront, was turned into a real triumph for them ; and it seemed as if they already were in possession of the crown which still awaited them. Some prayed, others were rapt in silent contemplation, but Petrus Baptista, who was in front, and Paulus Michi, who was in the rear, constantly preached to the people, exhorting and encouraging the Christians to perseverance, and entreating, with a valorous and pathetic voice, the heathens to embrace the Christian faith—the only way to their future and enduring happiness. These words made a very deep impression on the minds and hearts of the crowd. But the emotion of the sensitive Japanese was raised to its very highest pitch, and burst out into frantic expressions of compassion and pity, when they beheld the three little children, with their cheerful countenances, and heard them singing the praises of God, with their infantine and sweet voices, and saw their bleeding ears, which gave testimony of their sufferings. A nobleman was so moved in his heart that he approached the waggon and said to young Lewis: "My child, I will deliver you, provided you renounce your baptismal engagements." But the saintly Lewis courageously replied, "Not so : but you, also must become a Christian, for this is the only way to heaven—to eternal salvation." The zeal of the Christians, who accompanied the Martyrs, was so great that they freely approached the waggons and wiped off the blood from the Martyrs' ears ; crying aloud that they also were Christians, and that they desired to die the same death. Others hung their beads around their necks, and leaped upon the waggons, that they might provoke the officials to throw them into prison with the Martyrs, and to condemn them to die with the holy company. Then women, and even children, threw themselves upon the ground before the oxen and the wheels of the waggons that they might pass over them and bruise them ; and they constantly proclaimed aloud that they were Christians, and that they were desirous of shedding the last drop of their blood in defence of the only true religion. The soldiers found it a very troublesome task to remove those valorous Christians; and though their labours to clear a passage were incessant, the solemn procession could only advance by slow degrees. On all sides were heard cries of "Martyrdom"—"Martyrdom"—"Death for Jesus,"

" Death for our holy Religion"—" To heaven "—" To heaven."

Having now returned to the prison, the Martyrs leaped from their waggons, and then congratulated each other, for the honour which God had graciously conferred upon them of being permitted to suffer contumely for the name of Jesus. Though their journey had been a glorious triumph, and they saw the palm within reach, yet they knew that humility must be practised to insure the victory; therefore, they solicited each other's prayers that all might persevere to the very end. Blessed Paulus Michi, the Jesuit Father, approached Father Petrus Baptista, and tenderly embracing him he thanked him with many words, whilst his countenance was radiant with celestial joy. He humbly declared that it was to him a source of ineffable delight to find himself in such company, and that he highly appreciated the honour and the glory of finding himself and his two Brothers associated, on the road to martyrdom, with the worthy and zealous disciples of St. Francis. They again embraced each other, and, crying with holy joy, they separated. The soldiers and the drivers of the waggons, beholding those most extraordinary manifestations of joy in men so shamefully treated and condemned to death, said one to another:—" What men are these? From whence do they come? Where did we ever see men with such courage? Did we ever find men who rejoiced in humiliations and sufferings?"

The whole city was so excited that the Governor became alarmed; and, fearing that a general insurrection would arise, he proclaimed in all parts of the town that the decree only affected the Franciscan Fathers and the three Jesuits, and that no other persons should be molested. This news brought great affliction instead of joy to the Christians, who all wished to shed their blood for Jesus, and to seal by their death the firmness of their belief, and the sincerity of their conviction. They became disconsolate at the idea of losing the present glorious chance. Oh! how valiant are men made by the powerful aid of divine grace! Oh! what wonderful things are made easy of accomplishment to men whose hearts are centred in heaven, and whose souls are purified by the frequent worthy participation of the holy Sacraments of God's Church!

The Martyrs having, as we have said above, returned to their prison, after a little while Father Petrus Baptista addressed the following words to his Brethren :—" Where and how, my dearest Brethren, did we deserve the grace and honour which God has given us? We are now in the *royal* way, through which the apostles of Christ and other saints have walked, and have become worthy to occupy the seats which God had prepared for them in heaven. My dear children, what else can we expect after such a good and fortunate beginning, but an ending full of glory? Do pray to God for me that I may be worthy to be your companion in death, whom God had given to you for Father during life."

The Martyrs again consoled one another; they joined in the praises of God during the greater part of the night, and they again offered to God the sacrifice of their lives.

The next day, the 4th of January, the Martyrs were again brought out of their prison, and transported on horseback to Osaka, which is situated at the distance of eight miles from Miako. The streets and the highways, through which they passed, were all thronged with people, the great bulk of whom were Pagans, who came through curiosity. There were very many Christians there too, who still clung to their spiritual Fathers, asking for advice, or recommending themselves to their prayers, and in whom

I

the hope still lingered that they might yet be made companions in sufferings, and be joined in the struggle for the attainment of the palm of a glorious martyrdom. The old and pious Cosmas Joya ran in full haste to the gate of the town through which the Fathers had to pass, in order to receive their last blessing. The loud sobs of the dear old man moved the people to compassion, and the Fathers were struck by his great and constant fidelity. Father Petrus Baptista permitted the old man to take from him his Cross, which was still hanging on his breast, and was covered with his blood. Cosmas kissed the Cross, and kept this gift, more precious to him than gold, with the greatest care. He afterwards made use of it to encourage desolate Christians, who at the sight of the Cross remembered the good Franciscans—their advice, their labours, their zeal, their sufferings—and were thus encouraged to suffer more and more, and to remain, amidst all their trials, faithful to the end. As soon as the Martyrs arrived at Osaka, they were carried through the streets in the same manner as at Miako, and the same sympathy was shown to them. The Pagans themselves were heard saying to each other : " What a disgraceful and unjust proceeding ! What injustice and cruelty to those men who served our sick and miserable, and did no harm to any one ! " When they had thus been exhibited, the Emperor commanded that they should be conveyed by land to Nangazaki, in order to frighten the Japanese from receiving baptism, or giving hospitality to any Religious. It would have been an easier and much shorter route to send them by water to Nangazaki ; but the more they suffered, and the more publicity the story of their sufferings received amongst the Japanese, the more securely did the Emperor feel that the blow he was now inflicting, and which had for its aim and object the utter overthrow and ruin

of Christianity, would be certain to effect its purpose.
It really appears that by this time, all the good
qualities formerly observed in Taiko-Sama had left
him, and that now he only followed the natural bent
of his depraved inclinations, and exhibited the work-
ings of his fierce passions in their most brutal forms.
On the 9th of January, 1597, the Martyrs left
Osaka for Nangazaki; and on their journey they
passed through Sackae, Fugimen, Firengo, Cuxi, and
Fimexi. When they reached the last-named place,
they were still more than 100 miles distant from
Nangazaki. On their route they were always surrounded by armed guards, one of the soldiers going
before the Martyrs and carrying aloft the sentence of
death written on a scroll. The holy men suffered
intensely during their journey (which lasted a month),
from the brutality of their guards and from the
inclemency of the season, it being mid-winter. Nevertheless, at some places, they were well received by
the Japanese. It was during this journey that Cajus
Franciscus and Petrus Suchegiro, the two faithful
companions of the Fathers, were added to the society
of the twenty-four, thus making the number of
twenty-six complete. Our readers will remember
that Petrus Suchegiro had been selected by the
Jesuit Fathers to assist the holy Martyrs on their way,
as well as he could. The soldiers got tired of driving
him and his companion, Cajus Franciscus, back, and
at length they arrested both and placed them with
the others. Petrus Baptista enrolled them in the
Third Order of St. Francis, and they were filled with
unspeakable joy at finding themselves in the number
of the Martyrs, and on the eve of obtaining a share
in the same glory.

Father Martinus de Aguirre, in order to encourage
his Brethren and the others, spoke the following
words: "Brethren, let us reflect and remember that

we are great sinners, and, therefore, the favour which
God bestows upon us in this persecution, cannot be
sufficiently esteemed ; let us be thankful for this
blessing. Many Saints, like our holy Father St.
Francis, have desired to obtain the crown of martyrdom, and have sought it with eagerness, and yet it
was refused to them. Their merits were greater than
ours, and yet we receive this wonderful favour. Jesus
Christ loved all his Apostles, and yet but few have
obtained the Cross. Some have had their heads
cut off; others have been burned to death, thrown
into boiling oil, or into frozen water ; others have
been cut to pieces, or have suffered by other torments ;
but *to us*, His unworthy servants, He has given the
Cross, that noble Sign of our Redemption, on which
the only Son of God has expired for our sins. O,
my dear brethren, what would our holy Father St.
Francis have given, what would he not have suffered,
to obtain the same happiness which awaits us ? O,
Glorious Patriarch, St. Francis, thank and praise
God for us, because He has bestowed this great
favour upon us ! My dear brethren, let us be prepared to suffer all torments with courage and perseverance, bearing in mind the sufferings of our Lord
Jesus Christ for us. He confers immense favours
upon us, for by one mortal sin we have deserved
eternal punishment in hell, and in His goodness, He
is willing to commute this pain by *a moment* of
suffering. Let us pray with confidence for perseverance. Let us have recourse to the Blessed Virgin,
our Glorious Patron St. Francis, and our Angel
Guardian, and all the saints of heaven to intercede
and to pray for us, that by their intercessions and
prayers we may be strengthened by God to persevere
to the end." Thus did those holy men, by mutual
exhortation, encourage each other, to the great confusion of the Pagans, who still continued to visit the

Martyrs in all the places through which they passed,
and to listen to their discourses. In many instances
the Pagans wondered at the sublimity of the doctrine
set forth by those holy strangers, and they came to
look upon it with great favour The Bonzes (seeing
that by the constant preaching of the Martyrs, and
by their appearance in places where the Christians
had been unknown,*the Christian faith was more
propagated than before—for the preaching of the
holy men had created an inquisitive spirit—every one
being anxious to know something of a doctrine and of
a religion which inspired their followers with such
zeal and energy) said that the decree of the Emperor
had done more harm than good to the Pagans, for
now every Japanese was becoming dissatisfied with his
own mode of worship, having heard something else
that appeared to him preferable to his own. This
opinion of the Bonzes was not far from the truth, for
it was indeed a matter of great surprise to see how
eager the Pagans were to know something more concerning the tenets of the Christian religion. But, it
was still much more surprising to behold the zeal of
the Christians, which glowed with ardour, and became
intensified at the sight of the holy Martyrs. Amongst
the Princes and Noblemen who desired to suffer for
it, there stood conspicuously Ucondino ; and the two
sons and the cousin of the Governor of Miako, who
entered into rivalship with each other for the honour
of martyrdom. These last were unmoved by the
tears as well as by the threats of their parents and
relatives ; they trampled upon the honours which
their kinsmen would lavish upon them, and despised
the promises of honours which the Emperor had
made ; in fact, they despised every thing, even life
itself, and they prepared themselves, by assiduous
and fervent prayer, and by the constant practice of
other good works, for the reception of the palm of

martyrdom, which they daily expected to obtain. The other Christians were not less zealous; they publicly carried about them their beads, their crosses, and other emblems of their faith, that they might be openly recognised as Christians, and might thus find an opportunity to shed their blood. Gracia, the Queen of Tango, was ready, with all the ladies of the court, to run to the place of sacrifice. The Governor of Facata, a town in the Island of Ximo, in Japan, had issued a decree, by which all Christians were commanded to bring their beads, crosses, statues, and all other emblems of the Christian faith, to him; and he put on their doors a small board with the figure of an idol, and some words written upon it, which the Pagans supposed to be of great power against accidents by fire and other misfortunes. But all the Christians unanimously refused to comply with the execution of this order, and preferred death to a return to the worship of idols.

The same firmness of conviction was exhibited by the Christians of Nozu, who, having received a warning from the Governor to renounce their faith, prepared each a Cross, to carry it on their shoulders, and to die upon it, deeming this the best answer they could give to that impious idolater. The Governor was so struck by this sight, that he allowed them to continue in their faith. The Christians of Tacacuqui, who were nearly all poor labourers, having heard that the Martyrs were going to be crucified, held a meeting, and there they unanimously resolved to rather die a thousand times than to abandon their faith. The same thing was done by the Christians of Beari, and the places in the vicinity of Miako. Young children of twelve, ten, and even eight years of age, seeing their parents prepare themselves for death, were not satisfied until they were assured that they should be allowed to die with them. Some parents were willing to send their children to their friends, living at a distance, that they might be placed beyond the reach of persecution ; but the children declined to be parted from their parents, declaring that they also were Christians and anxiously desired to die for their faith and holy religion. Touching, indeed, was the spectacle exhibited in the house of the pious Cosmas Joya. His wife, Maria, and their daughters, most bitterly lamented that they could not obtain the crown of martyrdom, and that they were not even permitted by the soldiers to follow the Martyrs to the place of their triumph. Thus, young and old, rich and poor, men and women, confessed Jesus Christ publicly, and were neither ashamed nor afraid of their good God and His holy law.

Who can help remarking the power of God's grace, enabling men, and even children, to offer themselves freely to be put to death ? O God, how strong is Thy grace ! O Religion ! what power you impart to the soul thoroughly convinced of the truth of the faith of Jesus Christ ! Holy Christians ! Holy Martyrs ! obtain for us the same strength. O holy and renowned Heroes of the Cross ! pray for the conversion of the Japanese, and of all sinners.; and pray incessantly for the illustrious Pius IX., whom God inspired to place you upon His holy altars !

CHAPTER XIII.

THE invincible heroes approached step by step to their last resting place on earth. On the 31st of January they reached Facata, in which town they were well received by the Pagans, who were edified when they saw the holy Fathers, and observed their meek and saintly demeanour. Fazamburo, who had been appointed by the Emperor to superintend the execution, was made acquainted with their arrival, and he immediately ordered fifty Crosses to be quickly prepared. At the sight of so many Crosses (a greater number than was needed) the zeal of the Christians was doubly increased. Everywhere they talked to each other of nothing but of the coming tragedy, and of those who would be so fortunate as to suffer death with the Fathers.

On the 1st of February they reached Carazu, which was distant about three miles from Nangoia, where Fazamburo awaited them with his soldiers. Those men, though naturally of a cruel disposition and of rough and uncouth manners, showed great compassion for the Fathers. Fazamburo did sincerely wish that the Emperor had appointed another in his stead for the office of head executioner on this occasion. He swore by all his idols that those Religious were pious persons, and that they had been unjustly condemned to death. He was particularly struck by the sight of the three young children—Lewis, Thomas, and Anthony—who were like innocent lambs brought to the slaughter-house; and who appeared from their age more fit to play and amuse themselves than to be condemned to death for their faith. He tried to seduce Lewis, but he was promptly repulsed; for the child courageously answered that he would rather die and go to heaven than be spared and be lost for ever. The Martyrs then continued their journey in the custody of a double guard. After the lapse of a few hours they reached Figen. From thence they wished to perform the remainder of the journey on foot, that they might be able to gather more merits. On the 4th of February they reached, through rough and difficult roads, Sinoncho, which is situated about twenty-nine miles from Nangazaki. At Sinoncho two Jesuit Fathers met them, namely, Fathers Pasius and John Rodriguez, whom the Vice-Provincial had sent into those parts to comfort the prisoners and to give them the last Sacraments. But Fazamburo had given orders to hasten their departure, and the Jesuit Fathers, who had been deputed by their Superior, could not possibly execute their pious commission. It was not without very great difficulty that Father Rodriguez obtained permission to see and embrace those holy men, who, though worn out by the fatigues - of the journey and the sufferings inflicted upen them, looked so amiable, so resigned, and so cheerful. The good Father Rodriguez told them, in a few words, the object of his mission; but he said that only one short moment had been given him to see them, He, however, hoped, he told them, that at Nangazaki he would be able to administer to them the last consolations of holy religion. They then embraced each other with the most tender affection, and poured out their souls in joyful and loving effusions of heart to the Great God, for all His gracious mercies. Father Petrus Baptista told, in a few brief sentences, the principal features of their journey, and then concluded with the following words :— " Being so hurriedly dragged to death, I fear that no other opportunity may be given to me, and, therefore, I, the Superior of the Franciscan Fathers in Japan, humbly, and with the utmost sincerity, in the name of all my Brethren, ask pardon of the Vice-Provincial and all the other Religious of the Order of the Society of Jesus, for the difficulties we may have brought upon them by our preaching, or otherwise ;" and then kneeling down he wept bitterly. On the other hand, Father Rodriguez, moved by this great act of humility, embraced and kissed Father Petrus Baptista with great tenderness, and on his side he asked pardon of the Franciscan Fathers for the pain they might have caused them by their advice, or otherwise. He excused the good and holy intention of the Franciscan Fathers, and commended their zeal. Having again embraced the Martyrs, and having spoken a few words of encouragement to all of them, the moment for the short interview elapsed. The two Jesuit Fathers then departed without delay for Nangazaki, in order to be ready for the fulfilment of the object of their mission, as soon as the Martyrs would arrive at the end of their journey. In the evening the holy prisoners were taken on board a ship, which was in readiness to transport them to the place of their final sufferings. Their hands were tied behind their backs, as usual, and a rough cord was thrown around the necks of those who were *not* Franciscans. It is impossible to guess why this ignominy was not inflicted upon the Franciscans. Their last night was spent in prayer and in singing the praises of God. After a few more short hours their struggles would be all over—they would then be altogether in the full enjoyment of the eternal bliss in heaven. When a short period of time had elapsed, they reached the harbour of Tonchizu, which was about three miles from Nangazaki. Here they passed the greater part of the night on board the ship. The weather was exceedingly cold, and the Fathers suffered very much in consequence.

Fathers Pasius and Rodriguez had arrived at Nangazaki, and they redoubled their entreaties with Fazamburo to allow some time to the Martyrs to make their confessions, and assist at the holy Sacrifice of the Mass. Fazamburo resisted their demands, saying that he was afraid of great excitement in the town; that he would be held responsible for all the troubles and commotions that might arise; that he had previously prepared a convenient place for the Martyrs in Nangazaki, but that having witnessed the arrival of a great number of Christians, who came pouring in from all quarters, he had altered his mind, and would not allow them to enter the town; but that the Jesuit Fathers would be allowed to see them in the small Chapel near the hospital, and that a short space of time would be given to them to speak to each other; that their interview, however, must be short, because he had given orders that all must be over before the Christians were aware of it. The Martyrs are again marched off, and they arrive early in the morning of the 5th of February within view of the town of Nangazaki; and in this place the Jesuit Fathers Pasius and Rodriguez met their dear and happy friends, and told them that the final day had come at last—the day of glory and triumph! All the Martyrs thanked God, because they had at length reached the object of their longing desires, and had been deemed worthy to be ranked amongst the heroes of Christianity.

It happened that all the Crosses were prepared in the town, and it was therefore necessary to have them conveyed to the place appointed for the execution. On the same morning the crew of the galleon came into the town. The Governor had issued strict orders that nobody should leave the town, and he placed strong guards at each of the gates. All those circumstances convinced the inhabitants that something of importance was preparing. Soon the rumour was spread abroad that the Martyrs had arrived on that very morning, and were then being crucified. The news was communicated with the rapidity of lightning to all the people of the town, and the Christians rushed forth with fearless courage to the place of martyrdom. The guards were powerless to withhold them, and neither threats nor caresses could stop their onward march. The rushing crowd became immense, and was increased at every movement. People flocked in from all the neighbouring places, and great excitement prevailed. The happy victims, who were about to be sacrificed, were in the meantime quietly receiving the last consolations of religion in the hospital of St. Lazarus. The two Jesuit Fathers heard their Confessions, and all devoutly prayed together. The Bishop of Japan was also in the town of Nangazaki; but, however great his desire was to see the Martyrs, he could not succeed in his attempts to get out of the town. Being each time driven back, he sent his episcopal benediction by some of his companions. The humble and saintly Petrus Baptista sent his best thanks and those of his Brethren to His Lordship, and asked pardon of him for all that he and his Brethren might have done to cause the least pain to him. ✦

The Portuguese went to visit the holy Martyrs, and brought with them some succulent food and all kinds of sweetmeats, and other delicacies. But the

Martyrs would not taste anything : they accepted the presents, however, and then distributed them amongst the soldiers, giving the choicest portion to those who had been the most unfeeling and cruel to them. They even availed themselves of this opportunity to thank the soldiers for their services, and they told them that they looked upon them as kind friends and great benefactors, because they were to be the instruments by whose means the gates of the eternal Paradise were to be opened for themselves.

Fazamburo had first ordered that the Martyrs should be crucified at the common place of execution ; but at the request of the Portuguese, who wished to build a Church on the spot of their martyrdom, the Governor changed his mind and appointed another place. He commanded his men to carry the Crosses to a hill which was situated between the town and the sea, directly opposite to the general place of torture.

The Crosses were nearly like that upon which our Blessed Saviour was crucified, except that the Japanese Crosses have another crossbeam at the feet, and a piece of wood in the middle of them, upon which the body of the sufferer can rest. The following is the mode used in Japan for putting criminals to death by crucifixion :—The Cross is placed on the ground ; the condemned is then stretched upon it, and is nailed to it with iron rings on his feet, hands, and neck. Sometimes they tie the body with ropes, and at other times they break the bones, to make the condemned suffer more acute pain and torture in dying. When the process of fastening has been concluded, they raise up the Cross and fix it in the ground. After that, one executioner (perhaps two executioners may be employed) advances, and with a sharp lance pierces the body from the right side to the left shoulder, so as to pierce through the heart. In the case of two executioners, the second drives his spear from the left side to the right shoulder, so that the spears form a cross in the body of the sufferer. In the case of the holy Martyrs, two executioners were employed, and, consequently, they were singly pierced with two lances. The firmness and perseverance of the Martyrs had now been sufficiently tried by all kinds of sufferings: the moment had arrived in which their sacrifice would be consummated. They reached the final spot, and immediately Fazamburo ordered the soldiers to surround the Martyrs, and to keep off the crowds of people who had congregated in immense numbers, and were gathering round the holy Martyrs. It was only by using great violence that they could separate the people from the Fathers, and beat them back, to keep open a space of ten yards to give room for the executioners to act their parts. The two Jesuit Fathers Pasius and Rodriguez entered the ring with the Martyrs.

The joy of the heroes had by this time arisen to the highest point, for now they were near the crown of martyrdom, it was within their grasp. Up to this time the fear of being delivered had checked their joy and delight; but now all doubt was removed. The glorious and illustrious Father Martinus de Aguirre, with a firm and sonorous voice, intoned the Canticle, "*Blessed be the Lord God of Israel.*" The blessed Father Petrus Baptista stood with his eyes fixed on heaven, and rapt in ecstatic prayer, his soul held sweet converse with God. The little Lewis asked where his Cross was, and as soon as it was pointed out to him, he leaped with much joy, then kissed and embraced it, and by his whole deportment showed how much delight he felt. It was at that moment that the little Anthony, who was not less courageous than Lewis, overcame most nobly and heroically the last feelings of nature. His father and mother ran over to their son, and they endeavoured by their prayers, their sobs, and their sighs, to induce Anthony to apostatise ; but the hero, endowed with more than human strength, replied that he must serve God rather than his parents, that he was happy in the thought that he was going to die for Jesus Christ, and that soon he would be enjoying the bliss of eternal life. Fazamburo, seeing the parents weep so bitterly, stepped forward and tried to induce Anthony to follow their advice. But he was as powerless as the parents, and his arguments produced not the evil intended ; for little Anthony was strengthened by the grace of God, and therefore no human power could move him. Thomas Cosacki, the other child, was equally firm. With an angelic countenance he complacently viewed the Cross which was prepared for him ; and he lovingly embraced it, because he knew that it was to be the potent key that in a few moments would unlock for him the gates of Paradise.

It is not surprising to find that whilst the three children were exhibiting such energy and fortitude, the other Martyrs should appear so calm and resigned in the midst of the glittering of weapons, the rush of people, the cruelty of the executioners, and at the sight of the instruments of their torture ; and that they edifyingly preserved that cheerful appearance which had for so long a time won for them the love of both Christians and Pagans.

They now cordially embraced each other, and encouraged each other with the soothing words of love divine, and then kneeling down at the feet of Father Petrus Baptista, they all received from him his last benediction. Father Petrus Baptista was so exhausted that he was scarcely able to stand on his feet. He asked to be shown his Cross, and he knelt down before it and poured forth his soul in silent prayer. He had always desired to suffer the most and the first, and he now asked as a favour to be permitted to linger in torture longer than his companions, that he might have the pleasing satisfaction of seeing them enter before him. On beholding his great eagerness to be stretched upon the Cross, every one of the spectators was moved to tears. And whilst he was employed in stretching out his right hand to be nailed with a ring to the Cross, he besought one of the executioners to nail him through the hands. "There," he said, pointing to the middle of his hand, "there you should drive the nail;" but he could not obtain this last favour; he, therefore, humbly concluded that it was on account of his great unworthiness that he was not privileged to imitate so closely our Divine Redeemer.

They all stood near their Crosses, and at a given signal the executioners (each Martyr had two executioners, as we remarked before) began their bloody work; and they were all simultaneously attached to their Crosses. The Crosses were promptly raised up and placed in their proper positions. At this sight a shudder ran through the people who stood by. They witnessed this sad tragedy with horror, and by inexpressible but most significant signs, they showed that they wholly disapproved of and reprobated the proceedings, and felt compassion and pity for the victims of an iniquitous law. Immediately all tongues became silent, and the crowds of people who, like the troubled waters of the ocean, had been heaving to and fro, became calm and motionless. The people, the soldiers, and the magistrates, stood as if panic-stricken; and the eyes of all in this mute crowd were instantly directed towards the little Lewis, who, with his sweet, angelic voice began to sing, from the bloody instrument of his passion, the soul-inspiring hymn, " *Laudate pueri Dominum*"—"*Ye children praise the Lord.*" At the sound of this charming melody, the listening crowds suddenly awaking as it were from a lethargic sleep broke silence, and, sending forth a cry from all their mouths, they prayed for grace for those holy Martyrs, but especially for the little children. At that moment the spears were seen to vibrate in the hands of the executioners, and an icy shudder ran through all the nerves of the spectators, who fervently and loudly repeated the names—Jesus, Maria. The sides of the holy Martyrs had been pierced, the blood had gushed forth, and their precious souls, too good, too noble for the earth, took their flight, and, borne on Angels'. wings, they were carried into heaven. The first who died was Philippus de Jesu, and the last was the glorious Chief, Father Petrus Baptista.

Thus died those glorious Martyrs who, by their triumphant victory, may well serve as an example of virtue for all Christians, and as a lesson of shame for the Pagans. O glorious Martyrs of Japan, pray for us !

The following is the order in which their Crosses stood in a semi-circular form :—

1—CAJUS FRANCISCUS.
2—COSMAS TACHEGIA.
3—PETRUS SUCHEGIRO.
4—MICHAEL COSACKI.
5—JACOBUS KISAI.
6—PAULUS MICHI.
7—JOANNES GOTO.
8—PAULUS IBARCHI.
9—LEWIS.
10—ANTHONY.
11—PETRUS BAPTISTA.
12—MARTINUS DE AGUIRRE.
13—PHILIPPUS A JESU.
14—GONSALVUS GARCIA.
15—FRANCISCUS BLANCO.
16—FRANCISCUS PARILLA.
17—MATHIAS.
18—LEO CARASUMA.
19—BONAVENTURA.
20—THOMAS COSACKI.
21—JOACHIM SACCACHIBARA.
22—FRANCISCUS A MIAKO.
23—THOMAS DANCHI.
24—JOANNES CHIMOIA.
25—GABRIEL.
26—PAULUS SUZUCHI.

CHAPTER XIV.

WHO could attempt to describe the deep sensation that was created at the moment when death released the holy Martyrs from their sufferings? Who could fathom the depth of that compassion which was felt for them? Or, who could have stood by without being greatly moved at beholding the sorrowful tears that streamed down the cheeks of the Christians, when they contemplated the cruel treatment which those innocent souls—those heroic Apostles—had received in the name of law and justice? Fazamburo was very well acquainted with the Christian doctrine, for he had formerly desired to be baptised, but having too great an esteem for worldly honours and patronage, he shrank back, fearing lest he might lose the friendship of the Emperor, whose favourite he was. This man was, however, much moved by the sight before him, and the sparks of faith began to re-kindle within him. Looking on the Martyrs in the agonies of death, he wept; but being unwilling to let his weakness be seen, he withdrew, and giving the command to a subaltern, he gave orders to him to see that the Emperor's decree was fully executed. He apologised to the Portuguese, and said, with signs of great sorrow, that he had been forced to execute the decree of the Emperor. A Japanese Christian, a nobleman by birth, threw away his sword, saying that a Christian was unworthy to wear it if he could not use it to protect his Fathers and Masters, who had brought to him the great gift of the Christian faith.

A third Japanese, witnessing the great joy and cheerfulness with which the Martyrs died, embraced a Portuguese, and acknowledged that he was a Christian, and had received the holy baptism, but that he had become an apostate, and had renounced his faith, and had even contributed very much to procure the death of the Martyrs; he said, moreover, that he was exceedingly sorry for what he had done, and that he wished to be again reconciled to the Christian Church.

The Christians of Nangazaki, and of the neighbouring places, came in such numbers that the files of soldiers and guards were broken through, and, not regarding the blows and kicks which the military inflicted, those zealous persons pushed straight forward to the Crosses, to gather the blood that streamed from the Martyrs' wounds. They reverently collected the precious liquid, and even dipped into it precious cloth of gold and silver; and he who could collect the greatest share, considered himself the most fortunate.

When any of the people saw a drop of blood on the ground, they carefully took it up, with the earth with which it was commingled. Some even cut pieces from the Crosses, if they saw them intinged with blood. The zeal of the pious Christians to have mementos of the Martyrs was so great, that they cut pieces from their clothes, and took the nails from their hands and feet. The Bishop of Japan, who, though prevented by the soldiers from assisting the Martyrs in their struggles, had witnessed the cruel proceedings from his window, was now permitted to satisfy his devotion. He reached the place of execution three hours after the holy men had expired, and falling on his knees before the Crosses, he poured forth his soul in prayer before God with very great devotion.

'As an innumerable number of persons, both Christians and Pagans, had collected together from all parts to honour the sacred remains of the holy Martyrs, the Governor thought it advisable to double the guard, and to issue an order at the same time to all the guards, that under the penalty of death they should not suffer a single body to be removed. It would appear that God permitted this order to be issued, that the soldiers might be eye-witnesses of the wonders which He intended to operate for the renown of His Martyrs.

All the Christians were greatly strengthened by the death of the Martyrs. They did not fear the strong decrees which the Emperor had issued against them. The grand work of conversion now re-commenced, for the Pagans came in great crowds, having witnessed the calmness and cheerfulness of the Martyrs in the midst of the most excruciating pain, and the most debasing humiliations, to receive holy baptism, and be thoroughly instructed in the Christian faith. Thus again was verified the beautiful sentence of Tertullian : " *The blood of the Martyrs is the seed of Christians.*"

Eye-witnesses have reported several wonderful occurrences which happened in the places in which the bodies of the Martyrs had been exposed. We only refer to some of them, and that in a summary way, as those that have been approved of by the Apostolic See, as indubitable and authentic, will appear in the process of their Canonisation. Though strictly speaking there is no need for such proofs, it is sufficient that the Martyrs have sealed their faith by the copious effusion of their blood. This is the

principal point; and if God has been mercifully
pleased to manifest by some extraordinary prodigies,
the sanctity of His servants and the pleasure their
death for His sake has given Him, these are merely
proofs *ab extra*, which, though not strictly requisite,
serve as additional evidence. Perfection consists in
the love of God in the highest degree. The greater
the degree of love, the greater is the holiness of the
person. Jesus Christ, God equal to His Father, has
said that we cannot better show our love than by
sacrificing our own lives for Him whom we love. Let
us now relate a few of those wonderful occurrences.

On the Friday after their martyrdom, there appeared a column of fire above the Crosses, which
moved slowly round, and at last settled itself, for a
considerable time, above the hospitals, where the
Martyrs had practised so much charity. From the
hospitals it went to the little Chapel, and then disappeared. It is also recorded that on a certain day,
at twelve o'clock, noon, the body of blessed Petrus
Baptista disappeared from the Cross for a few hours,
and was afterwards seen again upon it.

Many weeks after his death this same body was
found incorrupt and fresh, as if it had only been
recently executed, and the blood was still observed to
run out. At another time, the Cross and the body
hanging upon it began to shake so violently, and for
so long a time, that the guards were greatly afraid.

Some authors also report that extraordinary signs
were seen in the air, which terrified the inhabitants
of Nangazaki, who thought that the tremendous Day
of Judgment had arrived. Many other wonders are
also reported, which we omit to describe in this
place.

As soon as the news of the death of the Martyrs
reached Manilla, in the Philippine Islands, the whole
city was filled with joy, and festivities on a large

scale were got up, because they had *new* saints in heaven, who had lived amongst them, and the people felt sure that they would pray for their friends here below. The Governor summoned his Council, and it was unanimously resolved that an Ambassador should be sent to Taiko-Sama to ask the reason why those holy men had been put to death, and also to reclaim their bodies. The Ambassador reached Japan in due time, and received from the Emperor this answer, namely: That he had put them to death because they had preached the Christian doctrine in his dominion, contrary to his orders. Taiko-Sama gave orders to the effect that the remains of the Martyrs should be given up to the Ambassador, who carefully gathered up those precious relics, and distributed the skulls to the Churches belonging to the Franciscans at Macao, Malacca, and Goa. All the rest he put into a large box; with those holy remains he placed the large board upon which was affixed the sentence of death, and he gave them to the Franciscan Convent at Manilla.

There was much excitement in Manilla on the arrival of the holy treasure. A solemn procession was ordered, which was composed of all the Clergy, both secular and regular, the civil authorities of the town, and all the inhabitants that were able to go abroad. Guns were constantly fired off, the bells rung their merriest peals, and the numerous bands of music made the air resound with their loud and jubilant airs. The procession started from the Cathedral, and moved along, through all the principal streets, to the Church of the Franciscan Fathers, where the martyrdom of their brethren was officially announced by archiepiscopal authority. All the vast congregation of people shouted out and loudly congratulated the Franciscan Fathers, because they had been so highly honoured as to be chosen by God to give the first Martyrs of Japan, and because they, and others of their brethren in distant places, were now enriched by the possession of the sacred relics of those sanctified men, who had watered the soil of that country with their sweat and blood.

CHAPTER XV.

BEATIFICATION OF THE MARTYRS.

THE Archbishop of Manilla and the Bishop of China and Japan, seeing the extraordinary devotion of the people, and knowing how much they honoured the memories of the Martyrs, and reflecting also on the cause of their death and martyrdom, resolved to investigate the matter canonically. They made a diligent inquiry, examined witnesses, and nicely sifted the evidence; and when they had brought their commission to a close, they sent a report to Rome, in order to obtain the beatification of those holy Missionaries.

Philip III., King of Spain, his Queen, Isabella, and a great number of the Spanish nobility also, asked the Pope and the Cardinals to investigate the matter thoroughly, and to grant the decree of beatification. The Pope and Cardinals were quite willing, and, therefore, in 1616, Pope Paul V. gave orders to three of the principal Members of the Rota in Rome, to begin the Process of the Beatification of the Martyrs. The three Commissioners chosen by the Pope were—Coccini, Manzanedi, and Pirovani, the last of whom died before the affair was completed, and Sacrati was named in his place. Farini was elected secretary of those three Commissioners. The usual caution of Rome in matters of such consequence, was observed in this matter. Letters were sent to all those places where the Martyrs had lived, and several judges were appointed to institute inquiries in them. Witnesses were called into court, and every one was allowed to make his deposition, and say whatever he remembered of the Martyrs during their lives. Amongst the Judges appointed were the Archbishop of Mexico, and another Bishop, who was a Suffragan of the Mexican Province; the Provincial of the Dominicans, and two Doctors of Divinity, the Vice-Provincial of the Jesuits, the Archbishop of Manilla, with the most learned of his Chapter, the Archbishop of Goa, and the Bishop of Macao. All these, with their several Reporters, occupied with joy the office committed to them, and began their labours with much scrupulosity of conscience. When all the necessary preliminaries were gone through, and all the documentary testimonials were collected together, they sent their report to Rome, accompanied with all the depositions of the several witnesses. Those documents, &c., were of considerable length, and it took the holy Congregation of the Rota a very long time to study and examine every particular circumstance. Their report was not sent in until after the lapse of several years, that is, in the Pontificate of Pope Urban VIII.

The Jesuit Fathers had on the roll-book of their Society, a long list of holy men who had suffered martyrdom in several other places, and whose beatification they had asked of the sacred Congregation; but they had not as yet thought of including their three members, who were martyred in Japan, together with the holy Franciscan Missionaries. However, the Minister General of the Franciscan Order reported the favourable turn of the matter with regard to the beatification of the Franciscan Martyrs, and insisted that the Superior of the Jesuits should lose no time to get the three Jesuits, who had suffered for the same cause, and at the same time, and under similar circumstances, included in the list. . He willingly agreed, and so the three Jesuits were included in the same decree of Pope Urban VIII., who, on the 14th of September, 1627, solemnly declared that the twenty-six Martyrs, who died by crucifixion for the Christian faith in Japan, were worthy of the honour of beatification, and also worthy of being honoured by all Christians. He fixed their Feast on the 5th of February, the anniversary of their death. He granted the office of the Martyrs to the Franciscan Order and to the Society of Jesus, and to the whole of the Clergy of the Diocese of Manilla.

Pope Clement XII. on the 13th of July, 1739, granted a plenary indulgence to all Christians who, on the Feast of the Martyrs, should visit the Churches of the Franciscan Order.

Thus has God been graciously pleased to honour His heroic servants here on earth; but who can describe the glory and honour they received in heaven, when they were met by the Immaculate Virgin Mother, all the celestial choirs of angels, and the glorious army of saints, who congratulated them upon their triumphant victory? Since the year 1608, many Franciscan Missionaries have gone out to Japan, under various disguises, to administer to the forlorn Christians the comforts of holy religion. Let us pray to those twenty-six holy Martyrs, that they may obtain from God for us, on this solemn occasion, all the blessings we stand in need of, and for the Japanese the grace to open their eyes that, seeing the impiety of their belief, they may embrace the truth in all sincerity. Let us further entreat them to obtain by their importunity before God's throne, that He would graciously inspire holy, zealous, learned, and indefatigable missionaries with the same zeal and the same sentiments as those with which He inspired Father Petrus Baptista; and that he would speedily raise up a body of men wholly regardless of self and burning with divine love, and prepared at all hazards to leave home and friends, and to carry the light of the Gospel even at the risk of their lives to those unfortunate people, who are sitting in the shadow of death, and yet were created for the same inheritance as we ourselves.

NOTE.—The last crowning act has just been performed in Rome, under the Dome of that magnificent structure which is sacred to God, under the Invocation of St. Peter, the Chief of the Apostles, the first Pope, and Bishop of Rome, by his saintly and illustrious successor, Pope Pius IX. Whit-Sunday, the 8th of June, in the year of Grace, 1862, will be ever memorable in the annals of God's Holy Church. The inhabitants of all the nations of the earth will, in generations yet to come, ever point with special delight to that remarkable day on which twenty-six glorious Martyrs of Japan, and one renowned Confessor, were placed by Apostolical authority, with the hearty concurrence of the universal Episcopacy (of whose number so very large a proportion was present), upon the Altars of the Catholic Church. "*Iniquity hath lied to itself,*" and bad men, inspired by human passion and assisted by infernal agency, have, in every age, been busily employed to undermine the foundations of that Divine Superstructure of which God Himself was the architect, and of which He is, and always will be, the Guardian and the Protector. Age after age has found men of that stamp, but they have always become unwittingly the instruments of fulfilling that double prediction of the Redeemer: "*the gates of hell shall not prevail against it*"—His Church. If the gates of hell cannot prevail against the Church of God; if they cannot succeed in their efforts to remove the "*Keystone of the arch*"—the Roman Primacy—then it is true to say, that as if in every age, from the very beginning, the impious and their retainers have laboured to overthrow the Church of the Living God, and to root out that Supreme Tribunal, whose judgments are final ("*Roma locuta est; causa finita est*"—St. Augustine), and have always miserably failed; so it will be true to say that the same agency will be at work, and the same results will follow, though sometimes the war will wage more furiously than at others, down to the last period of the world's existence; for the veracity of the Eternal Son of God stands pledged for the constant recurrence of scandals and persecutions, and also for not only their successive overthrows, but for their final extirpation. How grand must have been the spectacle witnessed in the glorious Basilica, on the anniversary of that great day, when the Holy Paraclete, who proceeds from the Father and the Son, descended upon the Apostles and those assembled with them! How magnificent must have been the scene! How grand the ceremonial! How venerable the hierarchy! How numerous the assemblage! How pious the aspirations! How consentient the approbation ! How glorious the results ! The large and benignant heart of the Sovereign Pontiff must have overflowed with delight when, looking down from his exalted throne, he beheld the numerous and venerable body of Cardinals, Bishops, and other dignitaries, with a long train of Clergy, both Secular and Regular, and tens of thousands of the faithful laity, representing all the nations of Christendom, blocking up that immense pile, which is at once a miracle of architecture, and a standing witness that God is ever present with His Church. Come forth, ye proud ones, and rival this magnificence, if you can. Come forth, ye rebellious ones, and justify, if you are able, your separation. Come forth, ye scoffers, and maintain your incredulity, in the presence of such solemnity, such grandeur, such zeal, such unanimity, such fidelity, such holiness, such undeniable proofs of the power of God, and of such miracles of grace. God is omnipotent, and He is immutable too, and His decrees will have their fulfilment in spite of human weakness and human perversity.

In the present work, we have only given a "Sketch" of the Lives and Acts of the illustrious Martyrs. We have made our book larger than we originally intended ; and as we have had less than a month for collecting our materials and putting them in condition, and have had, too, a multitude of indispensable duties to perform, we trust that our readers will overlook our defects and give us credit for good intentions. We were anxious to have the book on sale at the time of the Feast, and therefore we have no time to polish our style, and make our labours more acceptable. Want of time has also compelled us to omit many things which would tend to promote edification, and increase the knowledge of the bulk of our readers. But as we purpose shortly to publish a book having special reference to the labours of the Franciscan family, and in which all necessary information will be given relative to the great Indulgence of Portiuncula, which can be gained on the 2nd of August, by those worthily prepared, in all the Churches belonging to the Franciscans throughout the world—many things, now omitted for brevity's sake, will then appear ; and amongst the rest, a description of the Grand Ceremonial at St. Peter's, at which were present with the Holy Father, so many Ecclesiastical Dignitaries from all parts of the universe. We are Religious and invested with Sacradotal authority, but as we are bound by rule, we must act in the spirit of true obedience. Therefore, we submit our labours to the judgment of the proper tribunals, and we proclaim that we are prepared to submit with all humility to their decisions. We profess our unshaken belief in all the doctrines of God's One, Holy, Catholic, Apostolical, and Roman Church ; and, with the help of God's all-powerful grace, we are willing, like our martyred brethren of Japan, now enrolled amongst the saints, to suffer contumely, privations, and contradictions, for its sake, and even, if necessary, to shed our blood in its defence. The facts given in the present work, which we offer to the public, are chiefly taken from the old Flemish Chronicle of Fremant, one of the most accurate of historical writers of the Franciscan Order. We have also consulted the following, namely : L'Oliphants ; Lord Elgin's Mission to Japan ; A. Steinmetz's Japan and her People ; D. Bouix, Histoire des martyrs du Japon ; and the Geography of the Christian Brothers.

CHAPTER XVI.

THE royal Prophet David, after praising God with the most profound sentiments of adoration and thanksgiving, for the wonderful works, of His Providence in the creation and administration of the universe, raises his eyes above this material world, and the whole order of nature, to contemplate the new spiritual creation, and in a transport of admiration and thanksgiving cries out (in the 103rd Psalm, 30th verse), "*Thou shalt send forth Thy Spirit, and they shall be created: and Thou shalt renew the face of the earth.*" Of this new spiritual creation, the forming of the world out of nothing was but an emblem. This prediction and its accomplishment, this great and astonishing mystery; this wonderful work of the Holy Ghost; this new creation, as regards the establishment of the spiritual kingdom and Church of Christ on earth, and its propagation through all the nations of the known world, notwithstanding all the opposition that earth and hell could contrive against, are incontrovertible proofs of the divinity of the Catholic Church. The meridian sun could not appear clearer and brighter than the Divine Power and Wisdom did on this occasion; it shone in its full lustre, and confounded all the enemies of the Christian Religion, by such illustrious marks of supernatural interposition, and such incontestible proofs as no pretences could invalidate.

Christ, our Lord and Saviour, began to form His Church when He assembled His disciples and instructed them with His own mouth. Like a wise architect, he built His Church upon a firm rock, upon a solid and an immoveable foundation, that it should stand in spite of all storms, oppositions, or any efforts whatever to make it fall. His infinite wisdom did not use less prudence in the constitution of His spiritual kingdom than human legislators do in well-regulated states and societies, in which wise means are established to preserve economy, peace and tranquillity amongst the subjects. Magistrates are appointed to prevent confusion and disorder; judges are commissioned to give decrees, to interpret and explain the civil laws with sovereign authority, and to terminate the differences that arise between man and man, which otherwise might last till dooms-day, if every man was left at liberty to construe and expound the laws after his own fancy, or allowed to be judge in his own cause, and to prefer his own private interpretation to that of the unanimous decision of the whole body of judges and lawyers. Christ came, as He says Himself (St. John x. 16), to gather all the nations together, to bring back all who had been dispersed, that there might be but one sheepfold and one shepherd, one Church and one faith, as there is but one Lord and one baptism. It was His constant prayer, whilst on earth, that all His disciples should be one, as He and His heavenly Father were one (St. John, xvii. 21). He had expressed, in the most forcible terms (St. Matt. xii. 25), the desolation threatening a kingdom divided in itself. It cannot, therefore, be supposed that He would expose His own kingdom to such danger, or act in a manner that would not become any king or potentate on earth, by leaving His people without what is necessary to preserve subordination in every well-regulated society. He was sensible that no human means could contribute more effectually to cement unity in faith, subordination in government, peace and charity amongst Christians, and to preserve them from splitting and dividing into different sheepfolds or communions, than if He appointed a centre of unity, or an Universal Pastor over His Church, to regulate and govern it, and to influence all the particular churches in the world, as their visible Head, and Supreme Judge in matters appertaining to faith and morals.

In the Old Law the Jews had recourse to the High Priest of the Synagogue, in all matters of difficulty and importance, and they were obliged to submit to *his* judgment, though they had both the Scriptures and the Prophets (Deut. xvii). In the New Law, the Law of Grace, our Divine Legislator did not alter this method of instructing mankind. "*He chose one amongst the twelve Apostles,*" (says St. Jerome), "*as the visible head of His Church, that a head being appointed, the cause of schism might be removed.*" He commanded Peter to feed His sheep, and to feed His lambs, that is, His whole flock, without exception (St. John, xxi). He prayed for him, that his faith should not fail, and He left him as chief pastor of His fold to confirm his brethren (St. Luke, xxii. 31). He gave him in particular the keys of the kingdom of heaven (St. Matt. xvi. 19) as the ensign of supreme power and authority, which he communicated to him as His vicegerent on earth. In fine, He gave him the name of Peter, which signifies a rock, and declared that "*upon him, as a rock, He would build His Church, and that the gates of hell should not prevail against her,*" (St. Matt. xvi. 18). Hence the chief place in the sacred college of the Apostles was, from the beginning, assigned to Peter. In the enumeration of the twelve, *all* the Evangelists constantly place him in the front, and unanimously agree in naming him before all the rest, as the first. Our Lord usually directed His discourse to him, and he replied as the mouth of the rest, which made the primitive writers of Christianity constantly call Peter the Chief, the Head, the President, the Prolocutor, and the Foreman of the Apostles, with several other titles of distinction and prerogative.

Christ also appointed different orders of pastors, apostles, evangelists, and teachers to carry on the work of the ministry in succession, for the edification and preservation of His mystical body, and for conducting souls in the road of perfection (Ephesians, iv. 12). He authorised them to preach the Gospel (St. Matthew, x.), and gave them all the spiritual powers of the priesthood, to administer the Sacraments (St. John, xx. 21), *and to rule the Church of God, which He purchased with His own blood* " (Acts, xx. 28). He commissioned and sent them *" into the whole world"* (St. Matthew, xvi. 15), to teach all nations the same heavenly doctrine He had taught them ; to administer to them all the same baptism, and to establish one and the same plan of religious worship (St. Matthew, xxvii. 19). He, moreover, promised to " *send down the Holy Ghost to teach all truth* " (St. John, xvi. 1), and He assured them that He " *Himself would be with them all days, even to the consummation of the world;*" to assist them by the continual protection of His all-ruling Providence (St. Matthew, xxviii. 20), and, consequently, that he would be with their lawful successors in office, who are to continue to the end of the world, and to complete the work which they began ; for as the apostles neither did nor could teach all nations in their own persons, nor were to continue long on earth, it is manifest that the aforesaid commission and promises of Christ were not limited or confined to their persons, but were given and designed to extend to their successors in office. Here then we have just cause to admire the goodness of our Lord, who, requiring from us a belief of mysteries, which are above the comprehension of all human understanding, and founded in divine revelation, did not leave us trusting to the uncertainty of our own private judgment, or exposed to a variety of errors, and to an endless source of dissensions and divisions, but vouchsafed to provide us with a sure and an unerring guide, which is under the special protection of heaven, and the continual guidance of the Holy Ghost. Instead of a weak and blind reason, which we are to sacrifice in obedience to Him, according to St. Paul (2 Cor. x. 5), He was pleased to establish an authority that could not mislead us, and that every individual is bound to yield a firm assent to in religious matters. It was truly becoming the wisdom and worthy the goodness of Jesus Christ to preserve us thus from all illusions, differences, or disunions, with regard to our faith, and to secure us against all the doubts, fluctuations, and distrustful suggestions of an incredulous temper; to which they must be liable who shake off the yoke of authority to become their own guide in the affair of religion, as they can have no certainty that they are not misled by their own private opinion, and mistaken in their judgment—this being a thing that daily happens to thousands and thousands in cases less difficult and less abstruse than matters of faith. Every man of candour, who is open to conviction, must acknowledge that this method of instructing mankind by the authority of the Church, is the only sure channel through which the sense of revelation is conveyed to us with the most perfect certainty, and the best calculated rule for conducting us in the way of salvation, and for leading us to virtue and happiness in a plain, easy manner,

L

fitted to all capacities and adapted to the infirmities of human nature. By this means the ignorant, the dull of apprehension, and those, who through their weakness of understanding, and their several avocations, have not leisure, or are incapable of examining and interpreting the sacred Scriptures, or of judging for themselves, are instructed in the revealed truths; and have better eyes to see for them than their own. By this means also the learned, as well as the ignorant, are guarded against the illusions of pride and self-love, and furnished with the same motives of belief, and the same foundations for their faith. Instead of building on a sandy foundation, they build upon a rock, and have "*the pillar and ground of truth*" (1 Timothy, iii. 15), to support them; for which reason they are not to be shaken by all the specious arguments that human wit and learning are able to suggest. In hearing the pastors of the Church, they hear Jesus Christ Himself, who expressly says (St. Luke, x. 16), "*He that heareth you, heareth me; and he that despiseth you, despiseth me; and he that despiseth me, despiseth the Father, who sent me.*" In obeying the ordinances of the Church in matters concerning religion, they cannot go astray, since by that means they obey only the orders of Christ Himself, who says (St. Matthew, xviii. 17), "*He that will not hear the Church, let him be to thee as the heathen and the publican.*" Let us stop here, in silent raptures of astonishment, and briefly contemplate the spiritual beauty, incomparable advantages, and high prerogatives of the Church of Christ. She can never cease to be the true Church of Christ, nor can she fail in any of those sacred prerogatives with which Christ at first adorned her; she is always One, Holy, Catholic, Apostolical, and she always preserves the precious deposit of faith pure and unvaried. Christ always animates her by His Holy Spirit; He always presides over her as her Supreme Invisible Head; and *"as the vine communicates nourishment to the branches"* (St. John, xv) so He communicates to the members of His mystical body—the Church, the special influx of His gifts and graces, by the ministry He has established, and by the Holy Sacraments He has instituted for supplying all our spiritual necessities, and for healing all the disorders of our souls, that *" He might thus redeem us from all iniquity, and might cleanse to Himself a people acceptable, a pursuer of good works* (Titus, ii. 14); or, as St. Peter speaks (1 Peter, ii. 9), *" a chosen generation, a holy nation, a purchased people."* St. Paul assures us that Christ died for this very purpose, to purify His Church, and make her holy. *"Christ loved the Church,"* he says, *"and delivered Himself up for it, that he might sanctify it, cleansing it by the laver of water, in the word of life; that He might present it to Himself a glorious Church, not having spot or wrinkle, or any such thing, but that it should be holy, and without blemish"* (Ephesians v. 25).

To this Church all the nations of Christendom are indebted for their conversion, for their civilisation, and for whatever is good and useful in their institutions. This Church has been opposed by the world, in every period; but though her struggles were great, her triumph was certain. She has seen dynasties rise and disappear in rapid succession. Human philosophy and rebellious passions have singly and combinedly laboured for her ruin; but she has fought and conquered them, and shivered into infinitesimal fragments the puny instruments of their warfare. She is covered with the hoar of centuries, yet she is blooming with vigour and buoyant with hope; and as she has seen the end of her past, so shall she witness the destruction of all her future enemies. She alone has been the fruitful parent of Saints, whose number has been as countless as the stars;

she has illumined their minds, purified their souls, and inflamed their hearts; she has formed them to virtue, moulded their characters, fortified their labours, blessed their efforts, and crowned them with glory. She has blessed earth, made hell tremble, and peopled heaven with victors. She has consoled the poor, solaced the afflicted, curbed the haughty, checked the ambitious, terrified the tyrannical, mollified the hard-hearted, and spread light, and liberty, and justice, and faith, and love, amongst the inhabitants of a benighted world. It was she alone that could, and did, give to the world such heroic models as the Martyrs of Japan Their victory was a proof of God's Omnipotence, and her approval of their heroism is a proof of her heavenly origin, and that He who formed her will protect her to the end, and preserve her holy and undefiled on the earth, until the wreck of the world shall have brought time to a termination.

ERRATA.

.

Page 25.—For Tacuinus, read Jacuinus.

  „   36.—For *Nuntius,* read *Nuncius.*

  „   37.—For Camerines, read Camerino.

  „   39.—Before the words "moved his heart," in line 13 from the top, read "and."

  „   47.—After the words "subverted by them," in line six, read "he never would have persecuted the Christians."

  „   62.—For Toya, read Joya.

INDEX.

PRINTED BY A. IRELAND AND CO., PALL MALL, MANCHESTER.

www.ingramcontent.com/pod-product-compliance
Lightning Source LLC
Chambersburg PA
CBHW020545270326
41927CB00006B/726